Exercises to accompany

The Brief Handbook

Fourth Edition

The Brief Handbook Exercises

Fourth Edition

Kirszner & Mandell

Prepared by

Scott Douglass
Chattanooga State Technical Community College

Australia °°Canada°°Mexico°°Singapore°°Spain°°United Kingdom°°United States

THOMSON
HEINLE

The Brief Handbook, Fourth Edition
Exercises
Scott Douglass

Publisher: *Michael Rosenberg*
Acquisitions Editor: *Dickson Musslewhite*
Development Editor: *Julie McBurney*
Production Editor: *Lianne Ames*
Marketing Manager: *Katrina Byrd*
Manufacturing Manager: *Marcia Locke*
Compositor: *Nesbitt Graphics*
Cover Designer: *Brian Salisbury*
Printer: *West Group*

Printed in the United States of America.
3 4 5 6 7 8 9 10   06 05 04 03

For more information contact Heinle, 25 Thomson Place, Boston, MA 02210 USA,
or you can visit our Internet site at http://www.heinle.com

For permission to use material from this text or product contact us:
Tel   1-800-730-2214
Fax   1-800-730-2215
Web   www.thomsonrights.com

ISBN: 1-4130-0795-3

Contents

Name _____ Date _____ Score_____

Chapter 1   Exercise A
Getting Started

Consider a book that you have recently enjoyed reading.

1. How would each of the following writing situations affect the content, style, organization, tone, and emphasis of an essay about this book?

   • A journal entry recording your informal impressions of the book

   • An examination question that asks you to summarize the book's main idea

   • A book review for a composition class in which you evaluate both the book's strengths and its weaknesses

   • A letter to your local school board in which you try to convince your readers that, regardless of the book's style or content, it should not be banned from the local public elementary schools

   • An editorial for your school newspaper in which you try to persuade other students that the book is not worth reading

2. Choose one of the writing situations listed in number 1. On a separate sheet of paper, write an opening paragraph for the specified assignment.

Chapter 1   Exercise B
Determining Your Purpose

Consider an essay subject you have chosen or your instructor has assigned. How will your purpose and audience affect what you write and how your write?

1. Name your subject.

_____

2. What is your purpose?

_____

_____

3. Who is your audience?

_____

4. What will you write and how will you write?

_____

_____

5. On a separate sheet of paper, write your first paragraph.

Name _____ Date _____ Score_____

Chapter 1   Exercise C
Listing

Consider the variety of sources (such as people, books, magazines, observations, and so on) you encounter in a single day—sources that could provide you with useful information for the essay you are writing. In the space below, list ten of these potential sources.

1. _____

2. _____

3. _____

4. _____

5. _____

6. _____

7. _____

8. _____

9. _____

10. _____

Chapter 1   **Exercise D**
Freewriting

Begin with the most important sentence or idea in the paragraph you wrote in Exercise B, number 5. Freewrite until you have filled this page. If you wish, continue to freewrite on a separate sheet of paper.

_____

_____

_____

_____

_____

_____

_____

_____

_____

_____

Chapter 1   Exercise E
Brainstorming

Consider what you have discovered in Exercises B, C, and D. Do you
need to change any part of your plan for your essay?

1. Name your subject.

_____

2. What is your purpose?

_____

_____

3. Who is your audience?

_____

4. List all the points you can think of that seem pertinent to your
   essay.

_____

_____

_____

Chapter 1   Exercise F
Journal Entry

Write a journal entry evaluating your progress so far. Which of the strategies for finding something to write worked best for you? Why?

_____

_____

_____

_____

_____

_____

_____

_____

_____

Copyright © Heinle

Chapter 1   Exercise G
Cluster Diagram/Topic Tree

Review the work you did for Exercises B–F. Use this material to help you construct a cluster diagram or a topic tree. This exercise should help you to see how the ideas you have discovered can be organized into related groups

_____

_____

_____

_____

_____

_____

_____

_____

_____

_____

Chapter 1   Exercise H
Developing a Thesis

Analyze the following statements or topics, and then explain why none of them qualifies as an effective thesis. Be prepared to explain how each could be improved.

1. In this essay, I will examine the environmental effects of residential and commercial development on the coastal regions of the United States.

2. Residential and commercial development in the coastal regions of the United States

3. How to avoid coastal overdevelopment

4. Coastal development: pro and con

5. Residential and commercial development of America's coastal regions benefits some people, but it has some disadvantages.

6. The environmentalists' position on coastal development

7. More and more coastal regions in the United States are being overdeveloped.

8. Residential and commercial development guidelines need to be developed for coastal regions of the United States.

9. Coastal development is causing beach erosion.

10. At one time, I enjoyed walking on the beach, but commercial and residential development has ruined the experience for me.

Name _____ Date _____ Score_____

Chapter 1   Exercise I
Stating a Thesis

On a separate sheet of paper, formulate a clearly worded thesis statement for each of the following topics.

1. A person who has profoundly influenced the course of your life

2. Gun control and the Second Amendment

3. Should medical use of marijuana be made lawful?

4. Preparing for your retirement

5. The value of a college education

6. Public funding of the arts

7. Shoplifting

8. The role of cultural diversity

9. Parochial vs. secular education

10. Political correctness and the First Amendment

Name _____ Date _____ Score_____

Chapter 1   Exercise J
Stating a Thesis

Review the cluster diagram or the topic tree you made in Exercise G.
Use it to help you develop a thesis for an essay. Write your thesis in
the space below

_____

_____

_____

_____

_____

_____

_____

_____

_____

10   Copyright © Heinle

Chapter 1   Exercise K
Informal Outline

After reviewing your notes, prepare an informal outline for a paper on
the thesis you developed in Exercise J.

_____

_____

_____

_____

_____

_____

_____

_____

_____

Chapter 1   Exercise L
Rough Draft

Write a rough draft of the essay you have been planning. In the space provided, begin your rough draft. Then use your own paper to complete the rough draft.

_____

_____

_____

_____

_____

_____

_____

_____

_____

_____

Copyright © Heinle

Chapter 1   Exercise M
Collaborative Revision

After you have drafted a paper, form teams of two or three for collaborative revision. Read each other's papers and write responses to the "Questions for Collaborative Revision" below. Then discuss the comments.

- What is the essay about? Is the topic suitable for this assignment?

- What is the main point of the essay? Is the thesis stated? If so, is it clearly worded? If not, how can the wording be improved? Is the thesis stated in an appropriate location?

- Is the essay arranged logically? Do the body paragraphs appear in an appropriate order?

- What ideas support the thesis? Does each body paragraph develop one of these?

- Does each body paragraph have a unifying idea? Are topic sentences needed to summarize the information in the paragraphs? Are the topic sentences clearly related to the thesis?

- Is any necessary information missing? Identify any areas that seem to need further development. Is any information irrelevant? If so, indicate possible deletions.

- Can you contribute anything to the essay? Can you offer any ideas or examples from your own reading, experience, or observations that would strengthen the writer's points?

- Can you follow the writer's ideas? If not, would clearer connections between sentences or paragraphs be helpful? If so, where are such connections needed?

- Is the introductory paragraph interesting to you? Would another kind of introduction work better?

- Does the conclusion leave you with a sense of completion? Would another kind of conclusion be more appropriate?

- Is anything unclear or confusing?

- What is the essay's chief strength? What is its chief weakness?

Chapter 1   Exercise N
Customized Checklist

Using the revision checklists on pages 26–28 of *The* Brief *Holt Handbook* as a guide, create a "customized checklist"—one that reflects the specific concerns that are most important to you as you revise your essay. Then revise your essay according to this checklist. Use your own paper as necessary.

_____

_____

_____

_____

_____

_____

_____

After you have completed this revision, edit your essay and then prepare a final draft, being sure to proofread it carefully.

Chapter 1   Exercise O
Central Idea—Topic Sentence

The following paragraph is unified by a central idea, but that idea is not explicitly stated. After you have read the entire paragraph, identify the paragraph's unifying idea, write a topic sentence that expresses it, and indicate with a caret (^) where the topic sentence should be placed in the paragraph.

"Lite" can mean a product has fewer calories, or less fat, or less sodium, or it can simply mean the product has a "light" color, texture, or taste. It may mean none of these. Food can be advertised as 86 percent fat free when it is actually 50 percent fat. This "confusion" is considered acceptable because the term "fat free" is based on weight, and fat is extremely light. Another misleading term is "no cholesterol," which is found on some products that never had any cholesterol in the first place. Peanut butter, for example, contains no cholesterol—a fact that manufacturers have recently made an issue—but it is very high in fat and so would not be a very good food for most dieters. Sodium labeling presents still another problem. The terms "sodium free," "very low sodium," "low sodium," "reduced sodium," and "no salt added" have very specific meanings, frequently not explained on the packages on which they appear.

_____

_____

_____

Chapter 1   Exercise P
Central Idea—Topic Sentence

The following paragraph is unified by a central idea, but that idea is not explicitly stated. After you have read the entire paragraph, identify the paragraph's unifying idea, write a topic sentence that expresses it, and indicate with a caret (^) where the topic sentence should be placed in the paragraph.

The narrator in Ellison's novel leaves an all-black college in the South to seek his fortune—and his identity—in the North. Throughout the story, he experiences bigotry in a variety of forms. Blacks as well as whites, friends as well as enemies, treat him according to their preconceived notions of what he should be, or how he can help to advance their causes. Clearly, this is a book about racial prejudice. However, on another level, *Invisible Man* is more than the account of a young African-American's initiation into the harsh realities of life in the United States before the civil rights movement. The narrator calls himself invisible because others refuse to see him. He becomes so alienated from society—black and white—that he chooses to live in isolation. But, when he has learned to see himself clearly, he will emerge demanding that others see him, too.

_____

_____

_____

_____

Name _____ Date _____ Score_____

Chapter 2   Exercise A
Writing Descriptive Essays

Write the first paragraph of a narrative essay that retells a favorite short
story or fairy tale from memory.

_____

_____

_____

_____

_____

_____

_____

_____

_____

_____

_____

_____

_____

_____

_____

_____

_____

Chapter 2   Exercise B
Writing Exemplification Essays

Use the space below to write a paragraph discussing the merits of mov-
ies. Use at least three specific examples from your own experience to
support your thesis.

_____

_____

_____

_____

_____

_____

_____

_____

_____

_____

_____

_____

_____

_____

_____

_____

Chapter 2   Exercise C
Writing Process Essays

Think about your writing process. Then, explain your process as a set of instructions. Ask a fellow student to read and comment on your instructions.

_____

_____

_____

_____

_____

_____

_____

_____

_____

_____

_____

_____

_____

_____

_____

_____

Name _____ Date _____ Score_____

Chapter 2   Exercise D
Writing Cause-and-Effect Essays

The rights of adopted children are under a good deal of scrutiny lately. Although adoptees have long been denied information about their parentage, many people think they should have the right to know the identities of their biological parents. Write a paragraph that explores the possible effects on one of the following groups of opening adoption files: adoptive parents, foster parents, parents who give their children up for adopting, or adopted children.

_____

_____

_____

_____

_____

_____

_____

_____

_____

_____

_____

_____

_____

_____

_____

_____

Copyright © Heinle

Name _____ Date _____ Score_____

Chapter 2   Exercise E
Writing Comparison-and-Contrast Essays

Using the space below, compare any two athletes, movie or television stars, writers, or musicians.

_____

_____

_____

_____

_____

_____

_____

_____

_____

_____

_____

_____

_____

_____

_____

_____

_____

_____

Chapter 2   Exercise F
Writing Division-and-Classification Essays

Every social group is governed by a hierarchy, a system whereby individuals or groups of people are ranked at different levels according to
their relative importance in the group. Choose one group you know
well—your extended family, the population of your school, the people
in your neighborhood, fellow members of a special interest group to
which you belong, coworkers at your place of employment—and place
individuals within the hierarchy. Choose one of these individuals and
explain why they rank where they do according to your scheme.

_____

_____

_____

_____

_____

_____

_____

_____

_____

_____

_____

_____

_____

_____

_____

_____

Copyright © Heinle

Chapter 2   Exercise G
Writing Definition Essays

Choose a word or phrase that has a strong emotional meaning to almost everyone—patriotism or family values, for example—and interview five of your classmates asking each what the term means. Use their responses to write a definition of the word.

_____

_____

_____

_____

_____

_____

_____

_____

_____

_____

_____

_____

_____

_____

_____

_____

Chapter 3   Exercise A
Writing Coherent Paragraphs

Read the following paragraph and determine how the author achieves coherence. Underline parallel elements, pronouns, repeated words, and transitional words and phrases that link sentences. Label these devices in the margins.

Some years ago, the old elevated railway in Philadelphia was torn down and replaced by the subway system. This ancient El with its barnlike stations containing nut-vending machines and scattered food scraps had, for generations, been the favorite feeding ground of flocks of pigeons, generally one flock to a station along the route of the El. Hundreds of pigeons were dependent upon the system. They flapped in and out of its stanchions and steel work or gathered in watchful little audiences about the feet of anyone who rattled the peanut-vending machines. They even watched people who jingled change in their hands, and prospected for food under the feet of the crowds who gathered between trains. Probably very few among the waiting people who tossed a crumb to an eager pigeon realized that this El was like a food-bearing river, and that the life which haunted its banks was dependent upon the running of the trains with their human freight.

(Loren Eiseley, *The Night Country*)

Chapter 3   Exercise B
Writing Coherent Paragraphs

Insert missing transitional words and phrases to revise the following paragraph and make it coherent. Write your changes between the lines.

The theory of continental drift was first put forward by Alfred Wegener in 1912. The continents fit together like a gigantic jigsaw puzzle. The opposing Atlantic coasts, especially South America and Africa, seem to have been attached. He believed that at one time, probably 225 million years ago, there was one supercontinent. This continent broke into parts that drifted into their present positions. The theory stirred controversy during the 1920s and eventually was ridiculed by the scientific community. In 1954, the theory was revived. The theory of continental drift is now accepted as a reasonable geological explanation of the continental system.

Chapter 3   Exercise C
Coherence between Paragraphs

Read the following paragraph cluster. Then, on your own paper, rewrite the paragraphs and revise as necessary to increase coherence among them.

Leave It to Beaver and *Father Knows Best* were typical of the late 1950s and early 1960s. Both were popular during a time when middle-class mothers stayed home to raise their children while fathers went to "the office." The Beaver's mother, June Cleaver, always wore a dress and high heels, even when she vacuumed. So did Margaret Anderson, the mother on *Father Knows Best*. Wally and the Beaver lived a picture-perfect small-town life, and Betty, Bud, and Kathy never had a problem that father Jim Anderson couldn't solve.

The Brady Bunch featured six children and the typical Mom-at-home and Dad-at-work combination. Of course, Florence Brady did wear pants, and the Bradys were what today would be called a "blended family." Nevertheless, *The Brady Bunch* presented a hopelessly idealized picture of upper-middle-class suburban life. The Brady kids lived in a large split-level house, went on vacations, had two loving parents, and even had a live-in maid, the ever-faithful, wisecracking Alice. Everyone in town was heterosexual, employed, able-bodied, and white.

The Cosby Show was extremely popular. It featured two professional parents—a doctor and a lawyer. They lived in a townhouse with original art on the walls, and money never seemed to be a problem. In addition to warm relationships with their siblings, the Huxtable children also had close ties to their grandparents. *The Cosby Show* did introduce problems, such as so Theo's dyslexia, but in many ways it replicated the 1950s formula. Even in the 1990s, it seems father still knew best.

Chapter 3   Exercise D
Patterns for Paragraph Development

Determine one possible method of development for a paragraph on each of these topics. Then, on a separate sheet of paper, write a paragraph on one of the topics.

1. Depending on friends for transportation

2. An unexpected bill for automobile repairs

3. A perfect spot to take a vacation

4. Troubles that accompany being computer illiterate

5. The ideal campsite

6. The most useful software titles

7. The perils of not backing up computer files

8. The benefits of extracurricular activities

9. Jobs to avoid

10. The types of people who go to concerts

Chapter 3   Exercise E
Patterns for Paragraph Development

Read the following paragraph and then answer these questions.

1. In general terms, how could the paragraph be developed further?

2. What pattern of development might be used?

Civility once was considered the cornerstone of a progressive society. Disagreements were noted, but seldom publicly acknowledged. Violation of this custom among certain classes often resulted in the practice of dueling, which acted as a deterrent to uncivil behavior because of the finality of the outcome. Although dueling is now outlawed in our society, many disagreements are still settled through violence. The lack of civility remains problematic in our society.

Chapter 3   Exercise F
Patterns for Paragraph Development

Read the following paragraph and then answer these questions.

1. In general terms, how could the paragraph be developed further?

2. What pattern of development might be used?

Amish Friendship Bread is a culinary treat. It begins with the receipt of a gift of a batch of starter batter. The entire process—from receiving the batter to the finished product—takes ten days. The first day requires the addition of flour, milk, and sugar. Days two through five involve the once-a-day, gentle mixing of the batter. On day six, more milk, flour, and sugar are added. Days seven through nine repeat the daily mixing. On day ten, the long-anticipated outcome is realized as a portion of the batter is baked into a succulent loaf, while saving a starter batch to share with a friend.

Review Exercise A for Chapters 1–3
Writing Essays and Paragraphs

In the space provided, add further development to the ideas presented in the following paragraph. If you need additional space, complete the assignment on your own paper.

Most people look forward to vacations with great eagerness. Where they vacation, however, differs widely. Vacation locations depend on such factors as personal preference, financial considerations, and time available. Some people look forward to spending a few days in the mountains, while others can think of nothing more pleasant than sunning on a sugar-white beach. Regardless of their choices, vacations remain the goal and basis of fond memories for nearly everyone.

_____

_____

_____

_____

_____

_____

Review Exercise B for Chapters 1–3
Writing Essays and Paragraphs

In the space provided, add further development to the ideas presented in the following paragraph. If you need additional space, complete the assignment on your own paper.

    Young adults are social creatures. They enjoy gathering with others their age to celebrate various types of occasions. For example, an overnight tailgate party may precede a football game, or a group may gather for a clambake on a beach, or spring break may demand a special celebration. No matter the type of gathering, attention must be paid to details in order to make the celebration memorable.

_____

_____

_____

_____

_____

_____

_____

_____

_____

Chapter 4   Exercise A
Thinking Critically

Some of the following statements are facts; others are opinions. Identify each fact with the letter *F* and each opinion with the letter *O*. Then consider what kind of evidence, if any, could support each opinion.

1. The Charles River and Boston Harbor currently test much lower for common pollutants than they did ten years ago.

2. We no longer need to worry about environmental legislation because we've made great advances in cleaning up our environment.

3. The television rating system uses a system similar to the familiar movie rating codes to let parents know how appropriate a certain show might be for their children.

4. The new television rating system would be better if it gave specifics about the violence, sexual innuendo, and language content in rated television programs.

Copyright © Heinle

Chapter 4   Exercise B
Thinking Critically

Some of the following statements are facts; others are opinions. Identify each fact with the letter *F* and each opinion with the letter *O*. Then consider what kind of evidence, if any, could support each opinion.

1. The incidence of violent crime fell in the first six months of 1996.

2. New gun laws and more police officers led to a decrease in crime in 1996.

3. Affirmative action laws and policies have helped women and minority group members advance in the workplace.

4. Affirmative action policies have outlived their usefulness.

5. Women who work are better off today than they were twenty years ago.

6. The wage gap between men and women in similar jobs is smaller now than it was twenty years ago.

Chapter 5   Exercise A
Writing Argumentative Essays

For each of the following statements, list three arguments in favor and three arguments against.

1. Colleges and universities should provide free child care for children of currently enrolled students.

For _____

_____

_____

Against _____

_____

_____

2. Public school students should have to wear school uniforms.

For _____

_____

_____

Against _____

_____

_____

Copyright © Heinle

Chapter 5   Exercise B
Writing Argumentative Essays

For each of the following statements, list three arguments in favor and three arguments against.

1. Retirees earning more than $50,000 a year should not be eligible for Social Security benefits.

For _____

_____

_____

Against _____

_____

_____

2. The federal government should limit the amount of violence shown on television.

For _____

_____

_____

Against _____

_____

_____

Review Exercise A for Chapters 4–5
Critical Thinking and Argumentation

1. Read the following student paragraph and evaluate its supporting evidence.

The United States is becoming more and more violent every day. I was talking to my friend Debbie, and she mentioned that a guy her roommate knows was attacked at dusk and had his skull crushed by the barrel of a gun. Later, she heard that he was in the hospital with a blood clot in his brain. Two friends of mine were walking home from a party when they were attacked by armed men right outside the A-Plus Mini Market. These two examples make it very clear to me how violent our nation is becoming. My art professor, who is in his fifties, remembers a few similar violent incidents occurring when he was growing up, and he was even mugged in London last year. He believes that if London police carried guns, the city would be safer. Two of the twenty-five people in our class have been the victims of violent crime, and I feel lucky that I am not one of them.

Review Exercise A for Chapters 4–5 (continued)
Critical Thinking and Argumentation

2. In the space below, create your own version of an argument based on insufficient supporting evidence. As the topic for this paragraph, take a stance regarding the role that television has played in the pattern of declining scores on reading comprehension tests during the past twenty-five years.

_____

_____

_____

_____

_____

_____

_____

_____

Review Exercise B for Chapters 4–5
Critical Thinking and Argumentation

Revise the following draft of an argumentative essay, paying particular attention to the essay's logic, its use of support, and the writer's efforts to establish credibility. Be prepared to identify the changes you made and to explain how they make the essay more convincing. If necessary, revise further to strengthen coherence, unity, and style.

Television Violence: Let Us Exercise Our Choice

Television began as what many people thought was a fad. Now, over fifty years later, it is the subject of arguments and controversy. There are even some activist groups who spend all their time protesting television's role in society. The weirdest of these groups is definitely the one that attacks television for being too violent. As far as I am concerned, these people should find better things to do with their time. There is nothing wrong with American television that a little bit of parental supervision wouldn't fix.

The best argument against these protest groups is that television gives people what they want. I am not an expert on the subject, but I do know that the broadcasting industry is a business, a very serious business. Television programming has to give people what they want, or else they won't watch it. This is a fact that many of the so-called experts forget. If the television networks followed the advice of the protestors, they would be out of business within a year.

(This essay continues on the next page.)

Copyright © Heinle

Another argument against the protest groups is that the First Amendment of the US Constitution guarantees all citizens the right of free speech. I am a citizen, so I should be able to watch whatever I want to. If these protestors do not want to watch violent programs, let them change the channel or turn off their sets. The Founding Fathers realized that an informed citizenry is the best defense against tyranny. Look at some of the countries that control the programs that citizens are able to watch. In Iran and in China, for example, people see only what the government wants them to see. A citizen can be put into prison if he or she is caught watching an illegal program. Is this where our country is heading?

Certainly, American society is too violent. No one can deny this fact, but we cannot blame all the problems of American society on television violence. As far as I know, there is absolutely no proof that the violence that people see on television causes them to act violently. Violence in society is probably caused by a number of things—drugs, the proliferation of guns, and increased unemployment, for example. Before focusing on violence on television, the protestors should address these things.

All things considered, the solution to violence on television is simple: parents should monitor what their children watch. If they don't like what their children are watching, they should change the channel or turn off the television. There is no reason why the majority of television watchers—who are for the most part law-abiding people—should have to stop watching programs they like. I for one do not want some protestor telling me what I can or cannot watch, and if, by chance, these protestors do succeed in eliminating all violence, the result will be television programming that is boring, and television, the vast wasteland, will suddenly be turned into the dull wasteland.

Chapter 6   Exercise A
The Research Process

The following schedule will not only give you an overview of the research process, but it will also help you manage your time.

Activity	*Date Due*	*Date Completed*
Choose a Topic	_____	_____
Do Exploratory Research and Formulate a Research Question	_____	_____
Assemble a Working Bibliography	_____	_____
Develop a Tentative Thesis	_____	_____
Do Focused Research and Take Notes	_____	_____
Decide on a Thesis	_____	_____
Outline your Paper	_____	_____
Draft your Paper	_____	_____
Revise your Paper	_____	_____

Name _____ Date _____ Score_____

Chapter 6   Exercise B
Doing Exploratory Research and
Formulating a Research Question

List five subjects you want to know more about.

1. _____

2. _____

3. _____

4. _____

5. _____

Chapter 6   Exercise C
Doing Exploratory Research and
Formulating a Research Question

For each of the following, base your response on the list you created in Exercise B. Identify the subject by citing its corresponding number as it appears in Exercise B.

1. Which subject would be most interesting for you to do research and write about? Why?

_____

_____

_____

2. Which subject would be most interesting for your audience to read about? Why?

_____

_____

_____

3. Which subject would best lend itself to the assignment you have been given? How?

_____

_____

Copyright © Heinle

Chapter 6   Exercise D
Doing Exploratory Research and
Formulating a Research Question

For each of the following, base your response on the list you created in Exercise B. Identify the subject by citing its corresponding number as it appears in Exercise B.

1. For which of these subjects would you
   be able to locate the best source material?_____

2. Which subject do you choose? Why?

   _____

   _____

   _____

3. In the form of a question, record what you hope to find out by doing research and writing about this subject.

   _____

   _____

   _____

Chapter 7   Exercise A
Using and Evaluating Library Sources

List the reference books, bibliographies, periodicals, indexes, data-bases, and other resources that are related to your subject and available to you. Add to this list as you make discoveries in the course of your research and writing. Be sure to record all the information you will need for documenting your sources.

_____

_____

_____

_____

_____

_____

_____

_____

_____

Chapter 7   Exercise B
Using and Evaluating Library Sources

Search the resources that you identified in Exercise A. List the books, articles, people, organizations, and other material that you think will be most useful to you. Write a brief note to help you remember what you hope to learn or gain from each source. What do you expect each source to contribute to your research and paper? Revise this list as you continue to locate and evaluate source material. (Look ahead to Exercise C in this chapter and to Exercises A, B, and C in Chapter 8.) Be sure to record all information you will need for documenting your sources.

_____

_____

_____

_____

_____

_____

_____

_____

Chapter 7   Exercise C
Using and Evaluating Library Sources

Select one of the sources that you have identified (book, essay, or article from a newspaper, magazine, or journal), and then analyze its use of source materials.

1. What types of materials are used?

_____

_____

_____

2. Does the writer use more direct quotations than paraphrases? Are you able to determine why? If so, explain.

_____

_____

3. How does the writer give the reader a sense of the source's validity or credibility?

_____

_____

_____

Chapter 7   Exercise D
Using and Evaluating Library Sources

Select another of the sources that you have identified (book, essay, or article from a newspaper, magazine, or journal), and then analyze its use of source materials. (This repeats Exercise C, but with a second source.)

1. What types of materials are used?

_____

_____

2. Does the writer use more direct quotations than paraphrases? Are you able to determine why? If so, explain.

_____

_____

3. How does the writer give the reader a sense of the source's validity or credibility?

_____

_____

_____

Name _____ Date _____ Score_____

Chapter 8   Exercise A
Using and Evaluating Internet Sources

Using the Web browser that you prefer, enter a URL for one of the Web Sites found on pages 161–163 in *The* Brief *Holt Handbook.* Answer the following questions. Also, print at least the first screen of the Web site.

1. Does the site include a list of Contents that tells you the general topics? If so, what are the general topics?

_____

_____

2. Scroll to the bottom of the home page to locate the person responsible for managing the site (often referred to as the "Webmaster.") Is a name mentioned on this site?

_____

3. Does the site mention when it was last updated? If so, record it.

_____

4. Click on links to browse through the site. Is navigation easy? Is the site's organization easily understood?

_____

Copyright © Heinle

Chapter 8   Exercise B
Using and Evaluating Internet Sources
   Doing a Keyword Search

Using the Web browser and search engine that you prefer, complete the following tasks.

Type in: **Sistine Chapel**

1. How many documents are found?   _____

2. How are the listed documents sorted? (usually by relevance or site)

   _____

3. Are any of the listed documents commercial?   _____
   (Are they basically advertisements for a
   publisher, textbook, tour guide, or airline?)

   _____

4. Are any of the listed documents unrelated   _____
   to the Sistine Chapel? If so, estimate the percentage.

Chapter 8   Exercise C
Doing Your Own Keyword Search

Type in your own key word search on a topic of your choosing, revising the key words as necessary to obtain a manageable list of documents. Select one document, and then respond to these questions. Print at least the first screen of the Web site you select.

1. What is the source of the information?

\
\

_____

2. Is the Webmaster identified? Do you have reason to consider this author credible and reliable? Explain.

\
\

_____

3. Does the site mention when it was last updated? If so, record it.

\
\

_____

4. Does the text adhere to the conventions of research material that would be expected from print material? If so, briefly describe how the document meets those conventions. If not, what is lacking?

\
\

_____

5. Briefly evaluate the graphics, sound, or video. Are they used to enhance the text, or do they mask a lack of solid content?

\
\

_____

Name _____ Date _____ Score_____

Chapter 8   Exercise D
Citing Electronic Sources

Consult *The* Brief *Holt Handbook* and use proper documentation format for electronic sources to complete the following tasks.

1. Cite the source you used in **Exercise A: Using and Evaluating Internet Sources.**

_____

_____

2. Cite one source you located in **Exercise B: Using and Evaluating Internet Sources on the Web Doing a Keyword Search.**

_____

_____

3. Cite the source you used in **Exercise C: Doing Your Own Keyword Search.**

_____

_____

Chapter 9   Exercise A
Integrating Sources and Avoiding Plagiarism

Assume that, during your preparation for a paper on "the rise of suburbia," you encountered the following passage from the book *Great Expectations: America and the Baby Boom Generation* by Landon Y. Jones (New York: Ballantine, 1986). Read the passage and then, on your own paper, write a brief summary.

As an internal migration, the settling of the suburbs was phenomenal. In the twenty years from 1950 to 1970, the population of the suburbs doubled from 36 million to 72 million. No less than 83 percent of the total population growth in the United States during the 1950s was in the suburbs, which were growing fifteen times faster than any other segment of the country. As people packed and moved, the national mobility rate leaped by 50 percent. The only other comparable influx was the wave of European immigrants to the United States around the turn of the century. But as *Fortune* pointed out, more people moved to the suburbs every year than had ever arrived on Ellis Island.

Chapter 9   Exercise B
Integrating Sources and Avoiding Plagiarism

This is a continuation of the passage from *Great Expectations: America and the Baby Boom Generation* by Landon Y. Jones (New York: Ballantine, 1986). Read this portion and then, on your own paper, write a brief summary.

By now, bulldozers were churning up dust storms as they cleared the land for housing developments. More than a million acres of farm land were plowed under every year during the 1950s. Millions of apartment-dwelling parents with two children were suddenly realizing that two children could be doubled up in a spare bedroom, but a third child cried loudly for something more. The proportion of new houses with three or more bedrooms, in fact, rose from one-third in 1947 to three-quarters in 1954. The necessary *Lebensraum* could only be found in the suburbs. There was a housing shortage, but young couples armed with VA and FHA loans built their dream homes with easy credit and free spending habits that were unthinkable to the baby-boom grandpar ents, who shook their heads with the Depression still fresh in their memories. Of the 13 million homes built in the decade before 1958, 11 million of them—or 85 percent—were built in the suburbs. Home ownership rose 50 percent between 1940 and 1950, and another 50 percent by 1960. By then, one-fourth of *all* housing in the United Sates had been built in the fifties. For the first time, more Americans owned homes than rented them.

Chapter 9   Exercise C
Integrating Sources and Avoiding Plagiarism

This is a continuation of the passage from *Great Expectations: America and the Baby Boom Generation* by Landon Y. Jones (New York: Ballantine, 1986). Read this portion and then, on your own paper, write a brief summary.

We were becoming a land of gigantic nurseries. The biggest were built by Abraham Levitt, the son of poor Russian-Jewish immigrants, who had originally built houses for the Navy during the war. The first of three East Coast Levittowns went up on the potato fields of Long Island. Exactly $7900—or $60 a month and no money down—bought you a Monopoly-board bungalow with four rooms, attic, washing machine, outdoor barbecue, and a television set built into the wall. The 17,447 units eventually became home to 82,000 people, many of whom were pregnant or wanted to be. In a typical story on the suburban explosion, one magazine breathlessly described a volleyball game of nine couples in which no less than five of the women were expecting.

Chapter 9   Exercise D
Paraphrasing

In the space below, **paraphrase** the paragraph printed in Exercise C. If necessary, complete this assignment on your own paper.

_____

_____

_____

_____

_____

_____

_____

_____

_____

_____

Chapter 9   **Exercise E**
Quoting

In the space below, write a paragraph for a paper on "the rise of suburbia" combining summary, paraphrase, and quotation of the excerpts from *Great Expectations* that appear in Exercises A, B, and C. Be prepared to explain why you used summary, paraphrase, and quotation as you did.

_____

_____

_____

_____

_____

_____

_____

_____

_____

Chapter 9   Exercise F
Documentation

1. Insert the necessary MLA-style parenthetical citation(s) of source material into the paragraph you wrote for Exercise E. Publication information for *Great Expectations* appears in Exercise A. Assume that the page number you need to refer to is 27.

_____

_____

_____

_____

_____

_____

2. In the space below, write the entry you would use for *Great Expectations* on your MLA-style Works Cited page.

_____

_____

Review Exercise A for Chapters 6–9
The Research Process

In the space below, record five points with which you were familiar as you began this research unit, but which became more helpful after you had completed Exercises 6–9.

1. _____

_____

2. _____

_____

3. _____

_____

4. _____

_____

5. _____

_____

Review Exercise A for Chapters 6–9 (continued)
The Research Process

In the space below, record five points that were entirely new to you when you began this research unit, but now (after completing Exercises 6–9) you realize that they have merit and will likely prove helpful as you complete your next research assignment.

1. _____

_____

2. _____

_____

3. _____

_____

4. _____

_____

5. _____

_____

Name _____ Date _____ Score_____

Review Exercise B for Chapters 6–9
The Research Process

In the space below, record five points which you've found especially helpful and which you would offer as recommendations to someone new to the Internet.

1. _____

   _____

2. _____

   _____

3. _____

   _____

4. _____

   _____

5. _____

   _____

Review Exercise B for Chapters 6–9 (continued)
The Research Process

In the space below, record five problem areas which you've encountered
related to the Internet and which you would encourage others to avoid.

1. _____

_____

2. _____

_____

3. _____

_____

4. _____

_____

5. _____

_____

Chapter 10   Exercise A
MLA Documentation Style

For each of the following types of sources, provide a bibliographic entry that complies with MLA documentation guidelines.

A book by two authors

_____

_____

_____

An edited book

_____

_____

_____

An article in a monthly magazine

_____

_____

_____

Copyright © Heinle

Name _____ Date _____ Score_____

Chapter 10   Exercise B
MLA Documentation Style

For each of the following types of sources, provide a bibliographic entry that complies with MLA documentation guidelines.

A signed article in a newspaper

_____

_____

_____

A non-periodical publication on CD-ROM (such as Encarta®)

_____

_____

_____

A web page

_____

_____

_____

Chapter 11   Exercise A
APA Documentation Style

For each of the following types of sources, provide a bibliographic entry that complies with APA documentation guidelines.

A book by two authors

_____

_____

_____

An edited book

_____

_____

_____

An article in a monthly magazine

_____

_____

_____

A signed article in a newspaper

_____

_____

_____

Chapter 11   Exercise B
APA Documentation Style

For each of the following types of sources, provide an in-text citation that complies with APA guidelines.

A book by Shelly Fisher Fishkin entitled *Lighting Out for the Territory: Reflections on Mark Twain and American Culture* published in 1996.

_____

_____

_____

The first reference to a work by John Bogue, Mona Nichols, and William Blake published in 2002.

_____

_____

Subsequent references in the same paragraph.

_____

_____

The first reference in later paragraphs.

_____

_____

Name _____ Date _____ Score_____

Chapter 12   Exercise A
Chicago, CBE and other Documentation Styles

For each of the following types of sources, provide a bibliographic entry that complies with CMS documentation guidelines.

A book by two authors

_____

_____

_____

An edited book

_____

_____

_____

An article in a monthly magazine

_____

_____

_____

A signed article in a newspaper

_____

_____

_____

Review Exercise A for Chapters 10–12
Documenting Sources

The following notes identify sources used in a paper on censorship and the Internet. Following the proper format for MLA documentation, create a bibliographic entry for each source.

1. An essay by Nat Hentoff entitled Speech Should Not Be Limited on pages 22–26 of the book Censorship: Opposing Viewpoints, edited by Terry O'Neill. Greenhaven Press in St. Paul, Minnesota, publishes the book. The publication year is 1985.

_____

_____

_____

2. If You Don't Love It, Leave It, an essay by Esther Dyson in the New York Times Magazine, July 15, 1995, on pages 26 and 27.

_____

_____

_____

Review Exercise B for Chapters 10–12
Documenting Sources

The following notes identify sources used in a paper on censorship and the Internet. Following the proper format for MLA documentation, create a bibliographic entry for each source.

1. Terry O'Neill's introduction to Censorship: Opposing Viewpoints, found on pages 13 and 14. Greenhaven Press in St. Paul, Minnesota, publishes the book. The publication year is 1985.

_____

_____

_____

2. An essay in the Village Voice entitled The Speech Police Invade Cyberspace by Nat Hentoff. It was published on July 11, 1995, on pages 22 and 23.

_____

_____

_____

Chapter 13   Exercise A
Revising Sentence Fragments

The following passage contains fragments. On your own paper, rewrite the passage in complete sentences. Some of the fragments can be combined with independent clauses. For others, you will need to add a subject, a verb, or a new independent clause.

Today, more and more people are becoming interested in discovering their roots. Because of the popularity of a book by Alex Haley, called *Roots*. It tells the story of Haley's search for his ancestors. In Africa and other places. Before he wrote *Roots*, Haley worked on another book. *The Autobiography of Malcolm X*. After *Roots* was published. It became a bestseller. Then they made a movie for television based on it. Now, people of all backgrounds are interested in tracing their ancestry. A good book. A great man.

Chapter 13   Exercise B
Revising Sentence Fragments

The following passage contains fragments. On your own paper, rewrite the passage in complete sentences. Some of the fragments can be combined with independent clauses. For others, you will need to add a subject, a verb, or a new independent clause.

When we moved from an apartment to a house. We discovered that we had more belongings than we thought. So much stuff had to be packed. In the boxes. In suitcases. And even in large garbage bags. We rented a truck. From the local gas station. So we could avoid spending the extra money to hire a mover. We certainly put in a full day's work. That day. Although the process was long and hard. It was worth it.

Chapter 13   Exercise C
Revising Sentence Fragments

Use the conjunctions in parentheses to link the following short sentences or fragments. Rewrite and punctuate as necessary to generate a sentence that is smooth and correct.

Example: You should hurry. We are going to be late. (unless)

             Unless you hurry, we are going to be late.

1. The program aired. The executives had debated whether to release it. (after)

_____

_____

2. The dining hall serves three meals a day. Students must eat during the serving hours. (however)

_____

_____

3. The western cowboy. The frontiersman. Blend truth with American mythology. (both, and)

_____

_____

Chapter 13   Exercise D
Revising Sentence Fragments

Use the conjunctions in parentheses to link the following short sentences or fragments. Rewrite and punctuate as necessary to generate a sentence that is smooth and correct.

Example: You should hurry. We are going to be late. (unless)

             Unless you hurry, we are going to be late.

1. The officials did not like the thunder that shook the ground and lightning that brightened the sky. The soccer tournament was postponed until Saturday. (because)

_____

_____

2. Erica struck out eleven batters. She hit two doubles and drove in five runs. (not only, but also)

_____

_____

3. The administrators. The faculty. Correctly projected enrollment trends. (neither, nor)

_____

_____

Copyright © Heinle

Name _____ Date _____ Score_____

Chapter 14   Exercise A
Revising Comma Splices and Fused Sentences

Correct any run-ons or comma splices by inserting periods, commas, or semicolons as needed.

Example: The porch is sagging the window needs repair.

The porch is sagging; the window needs repair.

The porch is sagging. The window needs repair.

1. Linda is saving her money she wants to travel.

2. Brian could take Staci out for an enjoyable Mexican dinner and a movie he has enough money.

3. Clint and Ginger sold their television set now they do not miss it.

4. Don cleaned the apartment he cooked the dinner.

5. In graduate school, Louie once studied French and Spanish since then he has worked as a translator for the United Nations.

6. When the bridge closed, traffic was slowed for miles even leaving early did not help.

7. When you visit our campus for the interview, the most convenient parking lot is west of the building ask the attendant for directions to my office.

Chapter 14   Exercise B
Revising Comma Splices and Fused Sentences

In the space provided, mark a "C" for a complete sentence or "RO" for a run-on sentence. Draw a line between the independent clauses in run-ons.

1. _____ The president rose to speak, the audience listened.

2. _____ In the waiting room, one woman is writing a letter another reading a book about Chartres Cathedral.

3. _____ Brenda is actually the brain of the family's business, everyone should realize that by now.

4. _____ The group was small only twelve showed up.

5. _____ Answer, please, as soon as you can.

6. _____ The team has many talented players, Reece is the team's dependable shortstop.

7. _____ Ron built the deck, his craftsmanship is truly impressive.

8. _____ I am expecting a call has anyone telephoned?

9. _____ Johnny is respected for his attention to detail, each of his customers can be confident about the quality of work he provides.

10. _____ Last night I called you, I called several times.

Chapter 14   Exercise C
Revising Comma Splices and Fused Sentences

Correct these run-ons in each of the four ways you have learned.

1. Luke loves golf, he plays a round every sunny day.

a. _____

b. _____

c. _____

d. _____

2. Andy collects stamps he probably has that one.

a. _____

b. _____

c. _____

d. _____

3. Thomas enjoyed the sailboat he might buy a scooter.

a. _____

b. _____

c. _____

d. _____

Chapter 14   Exercise D
Revising Comma Splices and Fused Sentences

On your own paper, revise the following paragraph to change run-ons into complete and correct sentences.

Cats make great pets. You have to be affectionate to them. They are rather independent animals they do not always come when you call them. Many people prefer dogs, you can train them to come, or sit, or fetch a bone. With cats, on the other hand, you have to be willing to let them live their own lives if you attempt to train them you may become discouraged. If you put two cats in the same room, you are in for quite a treat. They chase each other, usually all in fun and when one catches the other the real show begins. Often they will cuddle and clean each other sometimes they will fight. The wise pet owner will know when to break up a fight and when to let it go since it is only play for the cats. They can be great company if you understand them.

Copyright © Heinle

Chapter 15   Exercise A
Revising Agreement Errors

Each of these sentences is correct. Read the sentences carefully and explain why each verb form is used in each case.

Example: *Pride and Prejudice* provides valuable insights about life in nineteenth-century England.

(The verb is singular because the subject *Pride and Prejudice* is a title of an individual work, even though it is plural in form.)

1. The children in the audience were mesmerized by the magician's entertaining illusions.

_____

_____

2. Mr. Reidinger's confidence in the benefits of Scouting activities has convinced him to serve as the scoutmaster, even though his son is no longer in the troop.

_____

_____

3. One look at their faces tells you that Angela and Erica enjoy playing softball.

_____

_____

Chapter 15   Exercise B
Revising Agreement Errors

Each of these sentences is correct. Read the sentences carefully and explain why each verb form is used in each case.

Example: *Pride and Prejudice* provides valuable insights about life in nineteenth-century England.

(The verb is singular because the subject *Pride and Prejudice* is a title of an individual work, even though it is plural in form.)

1. Although he fishes often with great success, Mr. Mims seldom comes home with a stringer because he considers "catch and release" to be sportsmanlike.

_____

_____

2. Every coach and player was pleased that the thunderstorm quickly passed through the area.

_____

_____

3. Aerodynamics is extremely important to bicycle design.

_____

_____

Chapter 15   Exercise C
Revising Agreement Errors

Write "C" if the sentence is correct or "X" if it contains an error in agreement. Rewrite incorrect sentences so that subjects and verbs agree.

_____ 1. They make good pizza here.

_____

_____ 2. Everybody know how to work together.

_____

_____ 3. The thunder and lightning was frightening.

_____

_____ 4. Either of the doctors can perform the surgery.

_____

_____ 5. Neither of the animals have been fed.

_____

_____ 6. Each member of the team has a uniform.

_____

_____ 7. You was an excellent worker on that project.

_____

_____ 8. Can you believe the pizzas was late?

_____

Chapter 15   Exercise D
Revising Agreement Errors

On your own paper, rewrite the following passage, changing the subject from a carpenter to carpenters. Keep in mind that verbs and other words that refer to the subject will have to be changed from singular to plural.

A carpenter uses many different tools in his work. When he is faced with a job that is particularly difficult, he has to use his patience as well as his skill. Without patience, a hammer, a saw, or a screwdriver will do a carpenter no good. He has to be able to understand the problem, and find the best way to solve it. Sometimes, the quickest solution is not the best one. His customer, or client, has to be pleased with his work, or he loses his chance to be hired for another job. There is a great pressure on the carpenter to succeed. By no means is his job an easy one.

Chapter 15   Exercise E
Revising Agreement Errors

Double the antecedent for the underlined pronoun in each sentence.

1. Leigh used <u>her</u> pen to write in her notebook.

2. Don wore a jacket over <u>his</u> sweatshirt.

3. Everyone at the party enjoyed <u>her</u> evening.

4. The car has a leak in <u>its</u> transmission.

5. The cow twitched <u>its</u> tail at the fly.

6. Aunt Peggy asked me to catch <u>her</u> dog.

7. My sister earned <u>her</u> doctorate at Florida State.

8. After Grace concluded her recital, the audience applauded <u>her</u> performance and hoped for an encore.

9. During winter snowstorms, the sparrows depend on our feeder for <u>their</u> food.

10. The rain fell throughout the afternoon; by supper, though, <u>it</u> had stopped, so we did not cancel our plans for the evening.

Chapter 15   Exercise F
Revising Agreement Errors

Complete each sentence by underlining the word or phrase that fits logically and clearly.

1. Thirty students have submitted (his/their) lab proposals.

2. Seconds later, Reece grabbed (its/his) backpack and ran.

3. With the hat, Andy wore (her/its) decorative headband.

4. Meg bakes bread that only (her/its) mother can rival.

5. Is Luke's car running (their/its) best this week?

6. My dog sleeps in (its/their) own cozy bed in the garage.

7. Idea became reality when Thomas used (its/his) brain.

8. Of the boys, Nat is most likely to have (his/their) work.

9. Spectacular views are Ronnie's goal on (his/their) hike.

10. Pleasure and confidence are (its/their) own rewards.

Chapter 16   Exercise A
Revising Awkward or Confusing Sentences

Review the following sentences for incorrect shifts in tense, person, number, voice, and mood. Underline the mismatched words.

Example: When I <u>tell</u> him that he is cute, he <u>grinned</u>.

1. I close the door because I needed to be left alone.

2. Bill wants to study medicine, but he dreaded the thought of four more years in school.

3. On our trip to Europe last summer, we stay at the best hotels, and we paid the highest prices.

4. Michael washed the dishes and then he begins to bake the cookies.

5. Ed runs well over one hundred miles each week and hoped to qualify for the Olympics.

6. When Reece entered the room, he adjusts the antenna and then changed the channel.

7. Anyone can learn French if they will only try.

8. After one is under water for ten minutes, they will have difficulty breathing.

9. If you adhere strictly to a vegetarian diet, one cannot eat steak, chicken, fish, or pork.

10. In her novel, Jane Austen creates a society that acts according to their characters' social expectations.

Chapter 16   Exercise B
Revising Awkward or Confusing Sentences

On your own paper, rewrite each of the following sentences in two ways to correct the shifts in tense, person, number, voice, and mood.

Example: When I <u>tell</u> him that he is cute, he <u>grinned</u>.
              When I tell him that he is cute, he grins.
              When I told him that he is cute, he grinned.

1. I close the door because I needed to be left alone.

2. Bill wants to study medicine, but he hated to think of four more years in school.

3. On our trip to Europe, we stay at the best hotels, and we paid the highest prices.

4. Michael washed the dishes and then he begins to bake the cookies.

5. Ed runs well over one hundred miles each week and hoped to qualify for the Olympics.

Chapter 16   Exercise C
Revising Awkward or Confusing Sentences

On your own paper, rewrite each of the following sentences in two ways to correct the shifts in tense, person, number, voice, and mood.

Example: When I <u>tell</u> him that he is cute, he <u>grinned</u>.
             When I tell him that he is cute, he grins.
             When I told him that he is cute, he grinned.

1. When Reece entered the room, he adjusts the antenna and then changed the channel.

2. Anyone can learn French if they will only try.

3. After one is under water for ten minutes, they will have difficulty breathing.

4. If you adhere strictly to a vegetarian diet, one cannot eat steak, chicken, fish, or pork.

5. In her novel, Jane Austen creates a society that acts according to their characters' social expectations.

Chapter 16   Exercise D
Revising Awkward or Confusing Sentences

On your own paper, rewrite the following passages to eliminate any incorrect shifts in tense, number, person, voice, or mood.

I work in a bank, and when you have that type of job, you have to be willing to wake up at a very early hour. Each morning, I drive to work, park my car, and walked a block to work. I get a lunch break every day at noon, and they love to eat at the delicatessen around the corner. I worked at the bank for over a year, and decided that I had had enough. After looking around for a new job, I found one where you had to be at work at 6:00 a.m. This job was in a restaurant where you had to stand up all day, and after six months, I decided to go back to the bank. The manager was very nice to me and says, "You can have your old job back if one promises to stay at least two years." I take the job, and I enjoyed an extra hour of sleep every morning.

Chapter 17   Exercise A
Revising Misplaced and Dangling Modifiers

In the space provided, write "C" if the sentence is correct as it stands. Write "DM" if it contains a dangling modifier.

1. _____ Shining brightly in the grass, she stooped to pick up the

silver coins that sparkled in the sunlight.

2. _____ While doing my homework, the supper burned.

3. _____ When you are ready, please drive me to school.

4. _____ Running to class, his digital clock pen was lost.

5. _____ The shirt is not only well made, but also attractive.

6. _____ Being antique cut-glass, she handled the bowl carefully as

she examined its intricate design.

7. _____ We saw three deer driving through the mountains.

8. _____ Having repaired the outside of the house, the inside needed

a great deal of attention as well.

9. _____ To play golf, the eye must be kept on the ball.

10. _____ I sat for an hour, waiting for the lights to go out.

Chapter 17   Exercise B
Revising Misplaced and Dangling Modifiers

On your own paper, rewrite each of the following sentences to correct any faulty modification.

Example: Increasingly concerned about the environment, conservation has become a hot topic.

Because many people are increasingly concerned about the environment, conservation has become a hot topic. (dependent clause)

1. Although a small part of the world's population, proportionally more of the earth's nonrenewable natural resources are used up by people in developed countries.

2. As fossil fuels, minerals, metals, timber, and water are diminishing, replacement cannot happen because they were built up over billions of years.

3. Doubling every decade, time for change of world consumption of oil would seem short.

4. By flooding certain coastal areas, seawater evaporation extracts a few minerals, such as common salt, magnesium, and bromine.

5. Although polluting the atmosphere, one-half to one-third of the world's additional energy needs in the next twenty years will be satisfied by the use of coal, according to experts.

Chapter 17   Exercise C
Revising Misplaced and Dangling Modifiers

On your own paper, rewrite the following passage, correcting any sentences that contain misplaced modifiers.

These days, many people are trying health foods in all parts of the country. The "back to nature" movement has nearly affected everyone in one way or another. Producers of health foods use no preservatives in their products which they claim are bad for the system. Cereals such as granola a totally natural food are especially popular. People are also eating unstarched rice which is supposed to be good for the digestive system particularly. Ice cream even comes in new, natural flavors such as banana and coconut which is made with fresh bananas. Certainly health food companies are trying hard to attract customers interested in better nutrition.

Chapter 17   Exercise D
Revising Misplaced and Dangling Modifiers

On your own paper, rewrite the following passage, correcting any sentences that contain dangling modifiers.

On arriving in America, the sights and sounds amazed Pierre. Having traveled alone, so many people hurrying around and shouting came as a jolt to him. Coming from a small village in the south of France, so much commotion had never before been witnessed by the young traveler. And being only eight years old and a bit nervous, his luggage seemed to be his only companion. On this trip, his cousins in Philadelphia would be his hosts. After looking for them at the gate, and not being able to find them, an attendant took him to the information booth. Over the loudspeaker, Pierre's cousins were paged. To locate them, an announcement had to be made twice by the attendant. Then, running through the terminal, from the other end of the building, Pierre recognized his relatives. Feeling relieved, Pierre ran to them and escaped the crazy crowds of America.

Review Exercise A for Chapters 13–17
Common Sentence Errors

Label the type of problem found in each of the following entries. For
your labels, select from the following list:

comma splice	fused sentence
dangling modifier	agreement error
sentence fragment	

1. On the Philmont trek, each scout packed his own water supply,
   compass, and rain gear. Also a share of the troop's tents and
   cooking equipment.

   _____

2. Thomas loaded the bottles and cans into his new Porsche, which he
   planned to leave at the recycling center.

   _____

3. Luke has missed work for seven consecutive days, he's concerned
   that his job is in jeopardy.

   _____

4. Andy bunted safely three times in yesterday's game he also stole
   home to score the winning run.

   _____

Review Exercise A for Chapters 13–17 (continued)
Common Sentence Errors

5. Beth explained, speaking directly to her father, how well she had run her race at the track meet.

_____

6. History can be exciting and engaging too often it is presented in a boring manner.

_____

7. Our family was surprised as we drove through Badlands National Park, the bleak landscape was oppressive.

_____

8. One of my favorite cities in the world is Edinburgh. London, Paris, and Rome, too.

_____

9. Margaret watched the colorful sailboats taking an afternoon jog along the shore.

_____

Review Exercise A for Chapters 13–17 (continued)
Common Sentence Errors

After thoroughly stirring the batter, making sure that there aren't any lumps in it, two eggs should be cracked into a small bowl. Take care not to break the yolks, and there shouldn't be any pieces of shell in the bowl.

Next, separate the yolks with a small spoon, and store them, since they will not be added to the batter, in an appropriate container. Using a small fork to beat the egg whites will become frothy. Then, combine the egg whites with the batter, mixing them in completely. Preparing the egg whites in this manner, it seems like a waste of time when you could just toss them into the batter. But this way, the waffles turn out with a light texture on the inside and fluffy too.

By this time, the preheating of the waffle iron is probably finished. Some batter should be put in the waffle iron, filling all of the ridges of the iron's bottom side, using a mixing spoon. Now, use a low, medium, or high setting to cook the waffle to your desired preference, golden brown, or for some, burned. These instructions will produce four medium-sized waffles.

Finally, the hardest part of preparing waffles is deciding what topping to use. Whatever topping you decide to use—fruit and cream, butter and syrup, or even ice cream—waffles are always a special, as well as a splendid addition to anyone's breakfast menu treat. Try them sometime.

Review Exercise B for Chapters 13–17
Common Sentence Errors

On your own paper, rewrite the following student draft to eliminate misplaced and dangling modifiers, faulty parallelism, shifts, mixed constructions, and faulty predication. Change and rearrange sentences as necessary.

Making Waffles

After a long night's sleep, how would you like to sit down to a cup of hot coffee and golden brown waffles for breakfast? You would probably like them with warm strawberries and a scoop of fresh, whipped cream, or you prefer the traditional butter and maple syrup. Waffles are, in any case, an excellent breakfast dish, and there are many ways to serve them, for they are easy to prepare. Basically, making waffles involves three steps: preparing the batter, cooking the waffle, and you have to decide how to top it.

First, before mixing the batter is where to preheat the waffle iron. Most irons have to be plugged in, and usually it took from ten to fifteen minutes to heat up. I have found that medium is usually the best setting, but which setting works best for you will have to be decided.

The batter is a relatively simple task. First, combine the following in a large mixing bowl: one cup of cake flour, two tablespoons of sugar, two teaspoons of baking powder, and finally add one-fourth teaspoon of salt.

Next, add one cup of milk and one tablespoon of vegetable oil to the dry ingredients. Oil is an important step; otherwise, the waffles will be stuck to the iron. If you don't have any vegetable oil, one tablespoon of melted butter or margarine can be used. Use a medium-sized spoon to stir the batter until it forms without any lumps in it a smooth mixture.

Review Exercise B for Chapters 13–17 (continued)
Common Sentence Errors

After thoroughly stirring the batter, making sure that there aren't any lumps in it, two eggs should be cracked into a small bowl. Take care not to break the yolks, and there shouldn't be any pieces of shell in the bowl.

Next, separate the yolks with a small spoon, and store them, since they will not be added to the batter, in an appropriate container. Using a small fork to beat the egg whites will become frothy. Then, combine the egg whites with the batter, mixing them in completely. Preparing the egg whites in this manner, it seems like a waste of time when you could just toss them into the batter. But this way, the waffles turn out with a light texture on the inside and fluffy too.

By this time, the preheating of the waffle iron is probably finished. Some batter should be put in the waffle iron, filling all of the ridges of the iron's bottom side, using a mixing spoon. Now, use a low, medium, or high setting to cook the waffle to your desired preference, golden brown, or for some, burned. These instructions will produce four medium-sized waffles.

Finally, the hardest part of preparing waffles is deciding what topping to use. Whatever topping you decide to use—fruit and cream, butter and syrup, or even ice cream—waffles are always a special, as well as a splendid addition to anyone's breakfast menu treat. Try them sometime.

Chapter 18   Exercise A
Using Verbs Correctly

Underline the correct verb in each sentence.

1. Although some floats (was/were) ruined by the downpour, the parade began as scheduled.

2. Everybody on the van (want/wants) an order of onion rings and a chocolate milk shake.

3. Although the variety of student backgrounds (make/makes) the class extremely challenging to manage, Mr. Hansard appreciates the stimulating and rewarding class.

4. Each member of the troop realizes that this Eagle Service Project (provide/provides) valuable service to the community.

5. Each member of the committee (has/have) been contacted by the secretary about the next meeting.

6. Many members of the board of directors (think/thinks) that the stock offering will be an immense success.

7. The competition is so keen that neither contestant (wants/want) to give her opponent an advantage.

8. To prepare for the competition, Erica and Beth (ride/rides) their bicycles several miles each day.

9. Every camper (enjoy/enjoys) "water balloon madness," which is the final activity on the first day of camp.

10. Each of the scholars on this school's Science Olympiad team (devote/devotes) a minimum of ten hours of preparation each week by surfing the Internet for helpful sites.

Chapter 18   Exercise B
Using Verbs Correctly

Underline the complete verb of each sentence.

1. Michelle and Mary moved to Hawaii three years ago.

2. Many people knit and sew their own toboggans.

3. There were shadows flickering in the firelight.

4. These candles could light the entire room.

5. Often, though, the candles sputter, flicker, and drip.

6. Jonathan Swift wrote *Gulliver's Travels*.

7. What else did he write?

8. Andrew and Jacob will be responsible for this project.

9. Hot peppers should be used sparingly.

10. What will the future bring?

11. Brian and Beth visited Yosemite National Park.

12. Every Beta Club member hopes to attend the baseball game.

13. Scouts could have served as guides along the path.

14. My computer has crashed only once this week.

15. Most students would prefer to purchase used textbooks.

16. The prowler has been seen in many areas of the neighborhood.

Chapter 18   Exercise C
Using Verbs Correctly

Underline the most logical verb form in each sentence.

1. Marjorie quietly opened the door, pushed her head inside, and (had looked/looked/will look) around the room.

2. If Diane (would have studied/studies/had studied), she would have passed the chemistry semester exam.

3. As you and Michelle must certainly know, for the past two hours I (am/was/have been) busy studying.

4. With several of his neighbors and fraternity brothers, Andrew (celebrate/celebrated/had celebrated) his birthday last night.

5. Before I head for class each morning, I eat breakfast, ride my bicycle, and (do/does/am doing) my exercises.

6. We will try harder, and we (do/did/will do) a much better job next time—if we get the opportunity.

7. The house (is built/was builded/was built) during the terrible heat wave last July and August.

8. Mary tossed the ball, and I (catch/catches/caught) it.

9. Only after he had arrived home from the store did Jacob realize that he (forgot/had forgotten/forgets) to buy bread, milk, eggs, yogurt, and a can of tuna fish.

10. After the performers had taken their final curtain call, the lights in the theater (dim/dimmed/had dimmed).

Chapter 18   Exercise D
Using Verbs Correctly

Complete each sentence by filling in the correct form of the verb in parentheses.

Example: We won the homecoming game last year,
              but we _____*lost*_____ (lose) it this year.

1. Mr. Hansard _____ (escort) a group of

   students to France last year, and he intends _____

   (take) another group to Spain next year. But Brian and Beth
   _____ (wait) one more year for his trip to
   Scotland and England.

2. After I had completed my lab report, I _____ (begin)
   to plan my English essay.

3. Elizabeth would have been prepared for the exam if she

   _____ (listen) to the lectures last week.

4. As I typed my research paper yesterday morning, my roommate's
   cocker spaniel _____ (sit) by my chair.

5. After my grandparents' television set was repaired,

   their stereo _____ (break) down.

Chapter 18   Exercise E
Using Verbs Correctly

Complete the sentences in the following paragraph by inserting the appropriate form (indicative, imperative, or subjunctive) of the verb in parentheses.

Harry Houdini was a famous escape artist. He _____ (perform) escapes from every type of bond imaginable: handcuffs, locks, straitjackets, ropes, sacks, and sealed chests underwater. In Germany, workers _____ (challenge) Houdini to escape from a packing box. If he _____ (can) manage to escape, they would admit that he _____ (be) the best escape artist in the world. Before getting into the box, he asked that the observers _____ (give) it a thorough examination. He then asked that a worker _____ (nail) him in the box. "_____ (Place) a screen around the box," he ordered after he had been sealed inside. In a few minutes, Houdini _____ (step) from behind the screen. When the workers demanded that they _____ (see) the box, Houdini pulled down the screen. To their surprise, they saw the box with the lid still nailed tightly in place.

Chapter 18   Exercise F
Using Verbs Correctly

Determine which sentences in the following paragraph would be more effective in the passive voice. Rewrite those sentences between the lines.

The Regent Diamond is one of the world's most famous and coveted jewels. A slave discovered the 410-carat diamond in 1701 in an Indian mine. Over the years, people stole and sold the diamond several times. In 1717, the Regent of France bought the diamond for an enormous sum, but during the French Revolution, it disappeared again. Someone later found it in a ditch in Paris. Eventually, Napoleon had the diamond set into his ceremonial sword. At last, when the French monarch fell, the government placed the Regent Diamond in the Louvre, where it still remains to be enjoyed by all.

Chapter 19   Exercise A
Using Pronouns Correctly

Underline the correct pronoun in each sentence.

1. The cat likes both Megan and (her/she).

2. Two were chosen, Bethany and (he/him), for the team.

3. Having appointed Beth as their representative, every member of the club was convinced that (her/she) would represent them well.

4. (He/Him) and Laura played soccer for the same high school.

5. It must be (he/his) car in the driveway.

6. The librarian checked out the videos to (me/I).

7. Royce hates broccoli; it must be (you/yours).

8. We wanted to go shopping with Nancy and (she/her).

9. I gave (he/him) the dog when we moved out of town.

10. Amy counts (they/them) among her best friends.

11. Don asked Amanda and (I/me) for our opinions.

12. The club decided to revise (its/their) schedule.

13. The band's producer and (she/her) have arrived.

14. Fortunately, it was (we/us) who heard the news.

15. The dean approved of (us/our) working together.

Chapter 19   Exercise B
Using Pronouns Correctly

Write a sentence using each of the following word pairs.

Example: computer   its

When the computer crashed for the seventh time this
afternoon, I simply pulled its plug and took a nap.

they   theirs

_____

_____

firefighter   who

_____

_____

technician   she

_____

_____

bicycles   their

_____

_____

Chapter 19   Exercise C
Using Pronouns Correctly

On your own paper, rewrite the following sentences, eliminating any faulty pronoun references.

1. We could not find a parking space, which was why we were late for the surprise party.

2. David told Eric that his acceptance speech was one of the best presented following the elections.

3. When Amy put the vase on the mantle, it fell down.

4. Backpacking is Allen's favorite outdoor activity. That is why he spends most weekends in the mountains.

5. When Beth sings that song, it drives her brother crazy.

6. Bev decided not to take the free ride on a hang glider, which allowed Gene to stop worrying.

7. Thomas told Luke that his brother had won first place in the contest for the most original Halloween costume.

8. Andy collects stamps, which provides him with a hobby that he shares with his grandfather.

9. The vocal group of residents convinced the company's board of directors not to build a factory near the town, which gave them a feeling of success.

Copyright © Heinle

Chapter 19   Exercise D
Using Pronouns Correctly

Underline the correct word in the parentheses.

1. The members of the singing ensemble agreed to wear (their/ they're/there) yellow toboggans for tonight's winter concert.

2. (Who's/Whose) team will win the tournament?

3. Who wrote "Beauty is (its/it's) own excuse for being"?

4. (Its/It's) puzzling that Chris hasn't been seen for several days.

5. Most of your classmates confuse you and (your/you're) twin.

6. Vince provided a model for (their/they're/there) design.

7. (Who's/Whose) sitting in that chair by the window?

8. The (governors/governor's) office has been evacuated.

9. (Womens/Women's/Womens') hats were far more popular in my grandmother's era.

10. Did you make a good grade on (your/you're) test?

Chapter 20   Exercise A
Using Adjectives and Adverbs Correctly

Underline the adjectives in the following sentences.

1. Clean air is essential if we are to have a safe environment.

2. On the lunar horizon, earth looms blue and cloud-streaked.

3. Whose car did you drive in this relentless downpour?

4. Lost and frightened children always arouse public sympathy.

5. This answer is correct, but that one is not.

6. Although his hair was gray, he was younger than he looked.

7. Did you leave your red umbrella at my house?

8. She was much taller than I.

9. His rumpled clothes and muddy shoes suggested that he had been walking for a long time.

10. The theater was crowded as the first showing ended.

Chapter 20   Exercise B
Using Adjectives and Adverbs Correctly

Complete each sentence by underlining the correct adverb in paren theses.

Example: The artful dodger dodged (<u>more artfully</u>/more artfullier) than the pursuer.

1. The (unique/most unique) shop opened last month.

2. Her embroidery is always (more delicate/more delicatest) than anyone else's.

3. Cindy became (more sick/more sickly) as the cruise continued into its third day.

4. Lynn is the (taller/tallest) of the two roommates.

5. Andy is (heavier/heaviest) than any other member of the state championship wrestling team.

6. Andy is the (heavier/heaviest) member of the state championship wrestling team.

7. David didn't act (grateful/gratefully) for the help.

8. Mocha is the (younger/youngest) of the six pups.

9. Ashley ran a (faster/more fast) mile than anyone else at the region track meet.

10. This unexpected winter storm is now (worse/badder) than it was an hour ago.

Review Exercise A for Chapters 18–20
Sentence Grammar

In the space provided, revise the following student draft to correct errors in pronoun use. Change words and phrases as necessary.

Duck, Duck Goose is a game that children play on a flat surface, usually outside in the grass so you do not get hurt. The first thing you need to do is to put them in a circle so them are sitting down. Choose one to be "it." They will be the first player to choose the "goose." The child whom is "it" will then go around the circle and tap everyone on the head. "It" will say "duck" when they tap them on the head except when they reach one—anyone who they choose. They will tap them on they head and say "goose."

_____

_____

_____

_____

_____

_____

_____

That's when the excitement begins. The "goose" will get up and chase "it" around the outside of the circle until they reach the place where "goose" was sitting and sits down. If "goose" tags "it" before "it" reaches the place where he was sitting, then they have to sit in the middle of the circle that they have made until someone else is tagged by a different "goose." When all of them have had the chance to be the "goose" and "it," then it can end.

_____

_____

_____

_____

_____

_____

_____

_____

Review Exercise B for Chapters 18–20
Sentence Grammar

On your own paper, revise the following student draft to eliminate incorrect, inconsistent, or ineffective verb use. Change words and phrases as necessary.

Dusty

On January 28, 1987, Dusty, my two-year-old Doberman pinscher, was born. Six months following his birth, I begun to train Dusty with Mr. Wagner, a professional dog trainer. After two weeks of obedience training, Dusty learned the "Heel" and "Sit" commands. We worked for four more weeks, spending thirty minutes a day on more basic obedience commands. Dusty, of course, responds very well. Not only he learned all of the obedience commands, but he and I had also built a strong relationship. We were best friends.

During the final week of training, Mr. Wagner says I done more and better with Dusty that he seen anybody else do with their dog since he was in the training business. He said, "I am proud of both your and Dusty's accomplishments."

I felt good about what I had done with Dusty and how all of those obedience commands had been learned by him. Dusty and I continued to work with one another for a year. During that time, he starts doing things that I had nothing to do with. For instance, he would attack anyone who threatens to harm me or anybody in my family. If my parents or brothers hit me whenever Dusty was around, Dusty attacks them. Should someone else hit a member of my family, Dusty attack that person. If you drove down our driveway and he didn't recognize your car, he run back and forth in front of it to make you slow down before to reach our yard. People whom he was not familiar with were not allowed to take one step out of their car. Dusty become very well mannered and protective of us.

A year and a half later, a tragedy happens. One summer day, my father is coming down the driveway in a different truck. Dusty hadn't really recognized who was driving the truck or the truck itself, so he darts out in front of it, trying to make it slow down before entering the yard. Unfortunately, the right front wheel hits Dusty in the hind leg and the right back wheel hit him in the head.

Fortunately, Dusty was still alive! No one was allowed to help him but me. Scared to death, I picked him up and he was put in the back of the truck. My second oldest brother rushed Dusty and me to the animal hospital. Dusty's blood is all over my hands and shirt, but I didn't care. All I want was for Dusty has the best medical care possible. Nearly crying, I lifted Dusty back out of the truck and take him inside the animal hospital.

After four days of treatment, the veterinarians allow me to take Dusty home, provided that he would be kept under close supervision. Limping away from the veterinarians, Dusty is eager to get home. It took another two weeks before he has totally healed. After his recovery was made, we continued his training, and he has made even more astonishing accomplishments. I am so proud of Dusty! Now that I am in college I miss him very much, but he will be seen again when I go home.

Chapter 21   Exercise A
Writing Varied Sentences

On your own paper, use coordination, subordination, and embedding to revise this string of choppy simple sentences into a more varied and interesting paragraph.

The Authorized Version of the Bible was first published in 1611. The Authorized Version of the Bible is often referred to as the King James Version. It involved several years of work by numerous scholars. Much of the year prior to its publication was devoted to final preparations. After it had been prepared, the document was sent to press. Many steps were taken during those final months. One step involved calling upon writers of the day. Several of the writers were eminent. They were needed to "refine" this translation. It was the most recent English translation. These writers devoted their efforts to the project. They enhanced the poetic qualities of Proverbs. They enhanced the poetic qualities of the Song of Solomon. And they enhanced the poetic qualities of the Psalms.

Chapter 21   Exercise B
Writing Varied Sentences

Complete each of the following steps on your own paper.

A. Combine each of the following sentence groups into one long sentence.
B. Then, compose a relatively short sentence to follow each long one.
C. Finally, combine all the sentences into a paragraph, adding any transitions necessary for coherence. Proofread your paragraph to be sure that the sentences are varied in length.

1. The King James Version of the Bible is the subject of many literary legends. One of the legends is intriguing. It alleges that Shakespeare's hand is present in the King James Version of the Bible. More specifically, though, it alleges that Shakespeare's hand is present in the 46th Psalm.

2. Count to the forty-sixth word from the beginning of the psalm. You will find that it is *shake*. Then identify the forty-sixth word from the end of the psalm. You will find that it is *spear*.

3. The situation becomes even more intriguing. It becomes even more intriguing when we realize that the revision work was underway in 1610. It becomes even more intriguing when we also realize that Shakespeare was forty-six years old in 1610.

Chapter 21   Exercise C
Writing Varied Sentences

On your own paper, revise the compound sentences in this passage so the sentence structure is varied and the writer's meaning and emphasis are clear.

Leonardo da Vinci's *The Last Supper* is one of the most easily recognized works of art. It was produced during Leonardo's residence in Milan. Leonardo was under the patronage of Duke Sforza. Leonardo used oil and tempera for *The Last Supper*. He used a wall in the refectory of Santa Maria della Grazie as his "canvas." Even the most casual art observer has viewed a copy of *The Last Supper*. But few serious students of art realize that it is actually a mural. It measures 14'-5" x 28'. It is surprising that Leonardo completed his work on such a large scale. It is surprising to many who have seen only small replicas. Many of these replicas are the size of a post card.

Copyright © Heinle

Chapter 21   Exercise D
Writing Varied Sentences

On your own paper, revise the compound sentences in this passage so the sentence structure is varied and the writer's meaning and emphasis are clear.

Giorgio Vasari records an interesting anecdote. Giorgio Vasari was an Italian art historian. He lived during the sixteenth century. The anecdote concerns Leonardo's use of models. These models were used for *The Last Supper*. Leonardo drew the disciples from life. Leonardo encountered difficulty in locating a suitable Judas Iscariot. While he worked on the painting, Leonardo met with some problems. Leonardo was troubled by the prior of Santa Maria. The prior monitored the work's progress. He monitored from a vantage uncomfortably close for Leonardo. The prior expressed his concerns to Duke Sforza. Leonardo heard that the prior had complained to the duke. Leonardo mentioned that any delay he had experienced was merely the result of his having encountered difficulty in identifying a model. The model was for the betrayer. Leonardo pointed out that he would be delayed no longer. He had located his model. The prior would serve nicely.

Chapter 22   Exercise A
Writing Emphatic Sentences

The following paragraph has both active and passive verbs. On your own paper, rewrite the paragraph using only active verbs.

Conestaga wagons are generally associated with the western frontier, but they were first used in Pennsylvania around 1725. Because heavy supplies were carried well by the wagons, they were used by settlers during the movement west. When the wagons were grouped for traveling, they were called wagons trains. In this way, the plains were crossed safely by many migrants. After the 1850s, the wagons were replaced by the railroads.

Chapter 22   Exercise B
Writing Emphatic Sentences

The following paragraph has both active and passive verbs. On your own paper, rewrite the paragraph using only active verbs.

When a European coast was landed on by the Vikings, fear of the Vikings' sudden and fierce raids was learned by the inhabitants. Their high-powered boats were sailed by these Norsemen from Scandinavia to the continent or Britain. The ships were decorated with striped sails and colorful circular shields. Little brightness was brought to the raiders' victims by these ships. A permanent mark was left on the territories that were attacked and occupied with ferocity and persistence by the Vikings. Particularly influenced by their customs and language were Norman France and the region of the British "Danelaw."

Chapter 23   Exercise A
Writing Concise Sentences

On your own paper, rewrite the following paragraph to eliminate wordiness.

When he first began writing, Samuel Clemens incorporated his own experiences that he had had. At one time he worked as a riverboat pilot on the Mississippi River. The pseudonym that he used as a writer, "Mark Twain," came from his experience during those days. This phrase was called out to mark the two-fathom mark on the riverboat line. When the Civil War started, it closed the river. Clemens could no longer pilot riverboats, so he moved west and became a newspaper writer. From his experience as a riverboat pilot, he took along his literary name.

Chapter 23   Exercise B
Writing Concise Sentences

On your own paper, revise the following paragraph to eliminate any unnecessary repetition of words or ideas. Also revise to eliminate deadwood, utility words, or circumlocution.

The seven daughters of Atlas are known as the Pleiades. They were pursued by Orion. Orion was unable to seize any of them. Orion continued to follow them. Orion continued to follow them until Zeus took pity on them. Zeus placed them in the heavens. Seven stars make up the Pleiades constellation. Only six stars are clearly visible. The seventh is invisible except for some people. These people are those who have especially keen vision. In Greek mythology, the seventh star represented Electra. Electra was the mother of Dardanus. Dardanus founded the Trojan race. There is a legend about Electra. The legend held Electra dropped from the sky. Electra did not want to look down from the sky. Electra did not want to see the destruction of Troy. Today, though, all seven stars are visible in the Pleiades. Actually, more than seven stars can be seen. But you must use binoculars to see more than seven stars in this cluster. You can even see several hundred stars. But you must use a telescope. Viewing through a telescope will yield several hundred stars.

Chapter 23   Exercise C
Writing Concise Sentences

On your own paper, revise the rambling sentences in the following
paragraph by eliminating excessive coordination and subordination,
unnecessary use of the passive voice, and overuse of wordy preposi-
tional phrases and noun constructions. As you revise, make your sentences more concise by deleting nonessential words and superfluous
repetition.

Orion lost the trail of the Pleiades. Orion became the companion

of Artemis. Artemis was a virgin goddess. Artemis was the goddess of

the moon. Artemis was also the twin sister of Apollo. Apollo feared

for his sister's chastity. Apollo sent a large scorpion to chase Orion.

Orion observed the scorpion enter a body of water. Orion pursued the

scorpion. Apollo then persuaded Artemis to shoot the object. The

object was bobbing in the waves. Her arrow pierced Orion's head.

Artemis was deeply saddened at her loss. Artemis placed Orion's image

among the stars. In the stars, Orion's image continues to be stalked by

the scorpion. The scorpion is also a constellation. Orion and the scor-

pion are separated. They are separated by a great distance. The Pleiades,

however, are in front of Orion. Orion is much closer to the Pleiades.

Orion continues to pursue the Pleiades.

Chapter 23   Exercise D
Writing Concise Sentences

Use sentence combining to rewrite the following paragraph on your own paper so that they are more concise and effective.

Shakespeare had a source for *Macbeth*. The story came from another book. That book was Holinshed's *Chronicles*. There Shakespeare found the tale. He found an account of King Duncan's murder. There he found a suggestion about Lady Macbeth. She was ambitious. There was the story of how Macbeth rose. It also included how he fell.

Chapter 24   Exercise A
Using Parallelism

Underline the word or phrase that maintains the parallel structure in each sentence.

1. At the party, Beth told us of her plans (to leave/and that she was leaving).

2. The more I think about the nuclear issue, the more one question (kept/keeps) entering my mind.

3. Whenever she has a spare moment, Kristi likes to read for entertainment and (enlightenment/to enlighten herself).

4. For months, Kathy's friends have told her that her boyfriend is lazy, poor, and (that he lacked education/uneducated).

5. In Whitney's first letter, she told us that her dormitory room is twelve feet long and (ten feet in length/ten feet wide).

6. Having just finished reading his favorite author's most recent novel, Vernon claims that it is brilliant, informative and (humorous/has a lot of humor).

7. My father likes (the country/to live in the country), to walk in the fields, and to fish in the streams.

8. (You are either late/Either you are late) or I am early.

9. Erica took up painting, writing, and (she taught/teaching) after she left the convent.

10. Dennis was surprised that Trish's favorite hobbies are swimming, playing the guitar, and (riding horseback/to ride horseback).

Copyright © Heinle

Name _____ Date _____ Score_____

Chapter 24   Exercise B
Using Parallelism

On your own paper, rewrite each of the following sentences in two ways, using effective and consistent parallelism in your revisions.

Example: Eat, drinking, and be merry.
                 a. Eat, drink, and be merry.
                 b. They love eating, drinking, and being merry.

1. Amy Rohling, one of the most talented people we know, is a painter, an actress, and who writes plays.

2. The camera takes clear pictures and that is easy to use.

3. Megan Nelson manages to hold a responsible position, earn an impressive salary, and she is writing a novel.

4. In the recording of popular music, the separate tasks of producing, arranging, and to engineer are often performed by one person who is called the producer.

5. When we are well rehearsed, when our timing is precise, and our singer is in good voice, we sound as good as any other band in the city.

6. On their first date, they were talking, ate, and drinking for hours after most others had left.

7. Laura refuses either to go by bus or by riding the subway.

8. Are marrying, child-rearing, and to shop all there is to life after graduate school?

9. At thirteen months, my grandson Michael exhibits remarkable agility of movement, he comprehends complex ideas, and aggressiveness of character.

Chapter 24   Exercise C
Using Parallelism

Identify the parallel elements in these sentences by underlining parallel words and bracketing parallel phrases and clauses.

Example: Each morning, my roommate amazes me with her energy: she [<u>wakes herself</u> at four o'clock without an alarm], [<u>jogs two miles</u>], [<u>cooks breakfast</u> for both of us], [<u>sends an e-mail</u> to her mother], [<u>calls her boyfriend</u>], and [<u>wears a smile</u> all the while].

1. Brian has developed a challenging training program: before breakfast, he jogs; after lunch, he bikes; and after supper, he swims.

2. Beth and Erica agreed that it was one of the best films they'd seen in several months: its characters were believable, its camera work was intriguing, its soundtrack was spectacular, and its language was inoffensive.

3. Angela worked all of her math problems, studied her Spanish assignment, read two history textbook chapters, and then wrote her composition.

4. Before making the long journey to Panama City Beach for spring break, take these precautions: change the oil, fill the gas tank, check the tires' air pressure, and replace the windshield wipers.

5. For a fishing trip that's certain to be memorable, my grandfather recommends the following preparations: pack your rod, reel, and tackle box; check the boat's motor; purchase gas and oil; and make plenty of peanut butter and jelly sandwiches.

Chapter 24   Exercise D
Using Parallelism

On your own paper, revise the following paragraphs, using parallelism and balance whenever possible to highlight corresponding elements and using repetition of key words and phrases to add emphasis. (To achieve repetition, you must change some synonyms.) You may combine sentences, and you may add, delete, or reorder words.

For hundreds and thousands of years, the Nile Valley experienced an annual flood. The yearly floodwaters of the Nile carried soil particles from upstream. The soil particles were deposited throughout the flood plain. The silt deposited by the yearly flood renewed the fertility of the Egyptian fields. This yearly event might be interpreted as a natural disaster. Rather than being a natural disaster, the annual flood permitted the rise of one of the richest of ancient civilizations. It was also one of the most advanced ancient civilizations. The annual flood enabled the people to grow enough food to support a large population. There was enough food for people for other activities. Some of these activities included building, scholarship, and art.

During the past century, the Aswan High Dam was constructed. There have been enormous changes in the Nile Valley. The Aswan High Dam is designed to retain an entire annual flow of the Nile. The Aswan High Dam also provides power to make cheap fertilizers. These fertilizers are needed by the intensively cultivated farms that are no longer covered by silty Nile water, which had previously renewed soil fertility. The Aswan High Dam has ended the annual flooding of the Nile Valley. The Nile used to bring nutritious silt to the region. The nutritious silt was once cherished for its nutrients. Many people now consider the silt a nuisance. The silt is considered a nuisance because it fills up irrigation canals.

Review Exercise A for Chapters 21–24
Sentence Style

1. Revise the following paragraph to eliminate awkward or excessive
   use of passive constructions.

Jack Dempsey, the heavyweight champion between 1919 and
1926, had an interesting but uneven career. He was considered one of
the greatest boxers of all time. Dempsey began fighting as "Kid
Blackie," but his career didn't take off until 1919, when Jack "Doc"
Kearns became his manager. Dempsey won the championship when
Jess Willard was defeated by him in Toledo, Ohio, in 1919. Dempsey
immediately became a popular sports figure; Franklin Delano Roose-
velt was one of his biggest fans. Influential friends were made by Jack
Dempsey. Boxing lessons were given by him to actor Rudolph Va-
lentino. He made friends with Douglas Fairbanks, Sr., and J. Paul
Getty. Hollywood serials were made by Dempsey, but the title his lost
by him to Gene Tunney, and Dempsey failed to regain it the following
year. Meanwhile, his life was marred by unpleasant developments such
as a bitter legal battle with his manager and his 1920 indictment for
draft evasion. In subsequent years, after his boxing career declined, a
restaurant was opened by Dempsey, and many major sporting events
were attended by him. This exposure kept him in the public eye until
he lost his restaurant. Jack Dempsey died in 1983.

Copyright © Heinle

Review Exercise A for Chapters 21–24 (continued)
Sentence Style

2. On your own paper, revise the following paragraph to eliminate deadwood, utility words, and circumlocution. When a word is superfluous, delete it or replace it with a more concise expression.

For all intents and purposes, the shopping mall is no longer an important factor in the American cultural scene. In the '80s, shopping malls became gathering places where teenagers met, walkers came to get in a few miles, and shoppers who were looking for a wide selection and weren't concerned about value went to shop. There are several factors that have worked to undermine the mall's popularity. First, due to the fact that today's shoppers are more likely to be interested in value, many of them have headed to the discount stores. Today's shopper is now more likely to shop in discount stores or bulk-buying warehouse stores than in the small, expensive specialty shops in the large shopping malls. Add to this a resurgence of the values of community, and you can see how malls would have to be less attractive than shopping at local stores. Many malls actually have up to 20 percent empty storefronts, and some have had to close down altogether. Others have met the challenge by expanding their roles from shopping centers into community centers. They've added playgrounds for the kids and more amusements and restaurants for the adults. They've also appealed to the growing sense of value shopping by offering gift certificates and discounts to shoppers who spend money in their stores. In the early '90s, it seemed as if the huge shopping malls that had become familiar cultural icons were dying out. Now, it looks as if some of those icons just might make it by meeting the challenges and continue to survive as more than just places to shop.

Review Exercise B for Chapters 21–24
Sentence Style

On your own paper, revise the following student draft to achieve greater sentence variety by varying the length, type, openings, and word order of the sentences.

A Cliffhanger

I slowly opened my eyes. I looked to my right. I could see the huge rocks. They lay awaiting a sacrifice fifty feet below. I looked to my left. I could see the questioning faces peering over the edge of the cliff. I could see snowflakes falling gently around me. Suddenly I came to a realization. Only one thing stood between the boulders and me. It was a gate. I came to another realization at that moment. I knew that skiing was not the sport for me.

It all happened one day in January. I had joined the school ski club. I still don't know why I had joined the ski club, but it seemed like a good opportunity to have fun and meet people. This was our first ski trip.

We rode on a bus to the ski lodge. The ride took an hour. During the ride, I began to worry. I wondered whether I would have been better off missing the trip altogether. I thought about everything that could possibly go wrong; I envisioned myself lying on a hospital bed. I envisioned doctors standing all around. They were trying to revive me. My friends had promised to teach me the basics of the sport. In spite of this, I could foresee a terrifying experience. I was right.

We finally reached the lodge. I decided to rationalize. I decided that this is skiing; it's supposed to fun. I was then feeling a bit courageous. I chose to begin on the intermediate slope. I went to the top of the mountain. I looked down the icy terrain. Visions of survival soon faded. A friend offered a few words of encouragement, and I began to conquer the mountain. I went down piece by piece.

I would ski about twenty feet at a time. Then I would stop. That way I would not pick up too much momentum. This process continued with healthy results. Then I reached one particularly demanding part of the slope. It consisted of a sharp drop. It was followed by a ninety-degree turn. I was looking at a deathtrap. It was waiting to engulf me. I said a quick prayer and pushed off. I did not know what lay ahead.

I handled the steep drop with minimal effort. My luck ran out as I attempted to turn. I tried to maneuver around an unsuspecting skier. I lost control. I could not turn. I veered off the ski trail. Of course, I collided with the poor man. I also bent his pole. This seemed trivial to me as I swiftly headed over the side of the cliff. I was in mid-air for a few seconds. I rushed head-on into a gate.

For a few seconds, I lay there in the snow. I was stunned. I did not realize what had happened. Then, I heard my friends calling my name. I heard spectators asking if I were alive. I came back to reality. I had risked my life. I had been participating in something most people call a sport. Fortunately, only my pride was bruised. I will never again slide down mountains on little pieces of wood.

Chapter 25   Exercise A
Choosing Words

On your own paper, rewrite the following paragraphs using standard English forms.

I rides the bus to school. Every morning I walks down to the corner where the bus stop. Usually the bus arrive every twenty minutes. Some days it come late. Yesterday, for example, I waits nearly thirty minutes until it arrived. Once I am on the bus, I usually watches the other riders. They reads they papers or looks out the window. Sometimes I reads until we reaches the campus stop. Then I gets off along with the other students, ready for the first class.

Chapter 25   Exercise B
Choosing Words

On your own paper, rewrite the following paragraphs using standard English forms.

Our neighborhood have many children. Every afternoon, the neighborhood children walks to the playground. If one child have a ball, all the childs tosses it around. If the swings be free, the Colton twins runs over to they. Other childs likes the slide or the sandbox. Although each child have a favorite activity, most of they does nearly everything before it get dark and they has to go home.

Chapter 26   Exercise A
Using a Dictionary

Use a college dictionary to answer the following questions about grammatical form.

1. What are the principal parts of the following verbs:

drink _____

deify _____

carol _____

draw _____

ring _____

2. Some of the nouns in the following list can be used as verbs. Underline those that can be used as verbs.

canter, minister, council, command, lord, minister, mother

3. What are the plural forms of these nouns?

silo _____

sheep _____

seed _____

scissors _____

genetics _____

alchemy _____

Chapter 26   Exercise B
Using a Dictionary

Use a college dictionary to answer the following questions about grammatical form.

1. What are the comparative and superlative forms of the following adverbs and adjectives?

<u>comparative</u>   <u>superlative</u>

fast _____

airy _____

mere _____

homey _____

unlucky _____

2. Are the following verbs transitive, intransitive, or both?

bias _____

halt _____

dissatisfy _____

turn _____

Chapter 26   Exercise C
Using a Dictionary

Use a college dictionary to find the restrictions on the use of the following words.

1. apse _____

2. bannock _____

3. flunk _____

4. irregardless _____

5. kirk _____

6. lorry _____

7. sine _____

8. whilst _____

Chapter 26   Exercise D
Using a Dictionary

Consult a dictionary to help you divide each of these words into syllables. Then indicate with a hyphen where you would divide each word at the end of a line.

Example:

underground   un • der • ground   under-ground

1. amazing _____

2. bookkeeper _____

3. calliope _____

4. longitude _____

5. markedly _____

6. martyr _____

7. side-splitting _____

8. thorough _____

9. transcendentalism _____

10. unlikely _____

Name _____ Date _____ Score_____

Chapter 26   Exercise E
Using a Dictionary

To test the research capability of your dictionary, use it to answer the following questions.

1. In what year did Anwar el-Sadat win the Nobel Peace Prize?

   _____

2. After whom was the Ferris wheel named?

   _____

3. What is the atomic weight of sulfur? _____

4. What is the full name of the French playwright known as Molière?

   _____

5. Define *surrealism*?

   _____

   _____

Chapter 26   Exercise F
Using a Dictionary

Using your college dictionary, look up the etymologies of the following words. How does the history of each word help you remember its definition?

1. mountebank

2. pyrrhic

3. pittance

4. protean

5. fathom

6. gossamer

7. rigmarole

8. maudlin

Chapter 27   Exercise A
A Glossary of Usage

Underline the correct word in the parentheses.

1. In ancient times, a comet signaled (eminent/imminent) danger.

2. The red convertible must have been going eighty miles per hour when it (passed/past) us on the freeway.

3. My dog (sits/sets) under our oak tree hoping to catch a squirrel.

4. The club's Code of Conduct embodies specific (principals/ principles) that each member is expected to uphold.

5. After asking for clarification on the point, the judge directed the attorney to (precede/proceed).

6. Kenjy's grandparents (emigrated/immigrated) from Japan.

7. Laura's recovery seems much (farther/further) along than the doctors had anticipated.

8. While some people are convinced that Kentucky's (capital/capitol) is Louisville and others thinks it's Lexington, you'll have to visit Frankfort to find the governor in the (capital/capitol) building.

9. Although the retired general has (less/fewer) power than he once possessed, he's fortunate that he also has (less/fewer) worries and obligations.

10. Did you make a good grade on (your/you're) test?

Copyright © Heinle

Chapter 27   Exercise B
A Glossary of Usage

Underline the correct word in the parentheses.

1. Although your essay is three days late, your instructor will probably (accept/except) it, but she'll likely penalize it.

2. If you want the penalty to have less (affect/effect), you should submit the essay as soon as possible.

3. (Who's/Whose) team will win the tournament?

4. Dee's poem makes an (allusion/illusion) to the seven deadly sins.

5. (Its/It's) puzzling that Mitzi hasn't been seen for several days.

6. Most of your classmates confuse you and (your/you're) twin.

7. Lochlin provided a model for (their/they're/there) design.

8. The three parties agreed (among/between) themselves to settle the case.

9. Kelsey's gymnastics coach (complemented/complimented) her for showing excellent improvement.

10. Hoyt has requested to remain (conscience/conscious) throughout the entire procedure.

Name _____ Date _____ Score_____

Review Exercise A for Chapters 25–27
Using Words Effectively

1. You've just returned from your month-long trip to the location of your choice. As a graduation gift, your wealthy aunt let you select your destination—anywhere in the world—and paid all of your expenses. In the space below, use diction appropriate for your friends to write a one-paragraph description of your vacation.

_____

_____

_____

_____

_____

_____

_____

_____

_____

_____

_____

_____

_____

_____

Copyright © Heinle

Review Exercise A for Chapters 25–27 (continued)
Using Words Effectively

2. In the space below, write another one-paragraph description of your vacation; in this account, however, use diction appropriate for your wealthy aunt, who wants to hear the details. Remember that she's former president of the local chapter of the Daughters of the American Revolution. By the way, when you're speaking with your aunt, two of her closest friends will be present in your aunt's parlor.

_____

_____

_____

_____

_____

_____

_____

_____

_____

_____

_____

_____

_____

_____

Review Exercise B for Chapters 25–27
Using Words Effectively

On your own paper, revise the following student draft for appropriateness, accuracy, and freshness. Where appropriate, include figurative language. Change words and rewrite sentences as necessary. [Note that this exercise continues on the back of this page.]

Pilot Mountain

My favorite place is a unique mountain surrounded by trees. Its beauty is better than all the modernization of man below it. It has a unique rock formation. Nowhere on this earth can you find another such creation that could even compare.

_____

_____

_____

_____

_____

_____

_____

_____

_____

_____

Review Exercise B for Chapters 25–27 (continued)
Using Words Effectively

The Little Pinnacle is where you want to look at the knob. Through all the mountain's original symmetry, the Little Pinnacle still remains the most breath-taking point. To reach this point, one must climb a long path full of lots of obstacles. After the hike one can rest on a rock and marvel at the wonders of nature.

_____

_____

_____

_____

_____

The most famous point on the mountain is the Knob. Looking from the Little Pinnacle, one can see lots of tall, straight trees growing on top of the Knob. The walls of the Knob are stone. No plants grow there. It all looks pretty funny. You can see the Knob from lots of other places in the area, but this view is still the best.

_____

_____

_____

_____

_____

_____

Chapter 28   Exercise A
Using End Punctuation

Correct these sentences by adding missing periods and by deleting unnecessary periods. If a sentence needs no changes, write *correct*.

Example: Dr Dan Drinnon examined his patient in the I.C.U. prior to recommending the emergency surgery

Dr. Dan Drinnon examined his patient in the ICU prior to recommending the emergency surgery.

1. Students are sometimes confused by the graduation requirements for the AA, the AS, and the AAS

2. Having gone through rigorous training, they were prepared now for their work in the Peace Corps

3. Have most of the faculty earned the M.A.?

4. After she graduated from F.S.U. with a J.D, she interviewed with N.A.S.A. in Florida with the J.P.L. in California.

5. The President's press conference at D.O.E. was scheduled for 10 am, but it was postponed until 2 pm

Chapter 28   Exercise B
Using End Punctuation

Correct the use of question marks in the following sentences. If a sentence needs no changes, write *correct*.

Example: Kate asked whether the game had been postponed because
             of the thunderstorm?

             Kate asked whether the game had been postponed because
             of the thunderstorm.

1. Lochlin wondered whether he should take a nine o'clock class?

2. The instructor asked, "Was the Spanish-American War a victory for
   America?"?

3. Are they really going to jump from that bridge???

4. Hoyt took a modest (?) portion of dessert—half a pie.

5. "Is *data* the plural of *datum*?," he inquired.

145

Chapter 28   Exercise C
Using End Punctuation

Correct the use of exclamation points in these sentences.

Example: Caught up in the excitement of the game, the announcer
                  shouted, "What a spectacular shot."

                  Caught up in the excitement of the game, the announcer
                  shouted, "What a spectacular shot!"

1. Are you kidding?! I never said that.

2. When the cell divided, each of the daughter cells had an extra
   chromosome!

3. This is fantastic. I can't believe you bought this for me.

4. Wow!! Just what I always wanted!! A red Mustang!!

5. "Eureka!," cried Archimedes as he sprang from his bathtub.

Chapter 28   Exercise D
Using End Punctuation

Add appropriate punctuation to this passage. Write your changes between the lines.

Dr Bertram Davis and his group of divers paused at the shore, staring respectfully at the enormous lake Who could imagine what terrors lay beneath its surface Which of them might not emerge alive from this adventure Would it be Col Jim Riser, chief scientist for the Royal Navy; Capt John Fenstermaker, the director of security at the naval base; or Dr Anne Rowe, author of numerous articles and books Or would they all survive the task ahead Dr Davis decided some encouraging remarks were in order

"Attention divers," he said in a loud, forceful voice "May I please have your attention The project that we are about to undertake—"

"Oh, no" screamed Col. Riser suddenly "Look out It's the Loch Ness Monster"

"Quick" shouted Dr Davis "Move away from the shore" But his warning came too late

Chapter 29   Exercise A
Using Commas

In the space provided, write "C" if the sentence is punctuated correctly or "X" if it contains an error in comma usage.

1. _____ They went to London, where they saw the queen.

2. _____ I called my sister last night and told her that I might be

   late for Thanksgiving dinner but I would be there before

   sunset.

3. _____ Before Richard knew it, the game was over.

4. _____ Until Matt decides to study, he will continue to fail.

5. _____ After he decides to study his grades will

   begin to improve.

6. _____ Although the salary is low, Joel likes to work.

7. _____ Although Cliff was much in debt, he entered the bank

   with the air of a conqueror.

8. _____ Kelsey tore up her first three drafts, because she

   wanted the letter to be perfect.

9. _____ The parlor, large and luxurious, was beautifully furnished.

10. _____ An old man, who had a broken leg, opened the gates.

Copyright © Heinle

Chapter 29   Exercise B
Using Commas

Insert any missing commas.

Example: My opinion inasmuch as you asked is that the expedition
            is likely to succeed.

            My opinion, inasmuch as you asked, is that the expedition
            is likely to succeed.

1. Beth's report made it clear that her four favorite artists are Monet
   Renoir Degas and Manet.

2. Let Brian and Angela our most skillful speakers present our
   proposal to the board of directors.

3. Long regarded as a leading newspaper the *Washington Post* boasts
   an outstanding staff of reporters.

4. Slowly slyly and cautiously Eric slid the wallet across the kitchen
   table.

5. During Louie's sophomore year in high school he read *As You
   Like It Julius Caesar Romeo and Juliet* and *Hamlet*.

6. I believe that is the book.

7. I believe that but it is an unusual excuse.

8. I believe that a dozen eggs will make quite a mess.

9. The elephant that stands on the drum is Maggie.

10. The elephant which is a hard worker and a talented performer is
    found in most zoos and circuses.

Chapter 29   Exercise C
Using Commas

The following sentences contain errors in the use of commas. Insert a comma as necessary. Circle any comma that should be deleted.

1. Once upon a time there was a dog that could fly.

2. We met as usual at the corner of Hollywood, and Vine.

3. I waited, for nearly a month for your letter.

4. It is my choice however to travel alone.

5. For once try studying.

6. You are mine and I am yours.

7. Write to me at 65 Market Street Portland Maine.

8. You are all prepared I'm sure for the test.

9. Ice cream if it is made at home is very good.

10. As long as I live I will love to dance.

Name _____ Date _____ Score_____

Chapter 29   Exercise D
Using Commas

The following sentences contain errors in the use of commas. Insert a comma as necessary. Circle any comma that should be deleted.

1. Waving her wand the good fairy performed some magic.

2. Never never will you get away with that.

3. I had a bacon lettuce and tomato sandwich for lunch.

4. Who in your opinion is the world's greatest athlete?

5. Her latest poem, is superb.

6. As of next week the prisoner will be a free man.

7. His answer which was wrong made the class laugh.

8. That dog barking at the tree, is mine.

9. We were wed on March 18 1939.

10. When our guests arrived we greeted them at the door.

Name _____ Date _____ Score_____

Chapter 30   Exercise A
Using Semicolons

Replace commas with semicolons where necessary to separate internally punctuated items in a series.

1. Research on animals' ability to think has been conducted on dolphins, who often respond to communicative gestures, sea lions, who seem to show some understanding of logical relationships between symbols, and parrots, who can be taught vocabulary.

2. Business letters should be written with a personal, courteous tone, best achieved through the use of the word *you*, a positive tone, easily created by rephrasing negative statements, and a natural tone, the result of using language that is intended to express, not impress.

3. Engaging in aerobic exercise results in benefits to the cardiovascular system, an increase in stamina, an important physical asset in today's fast-paced lifestyle, and an overall sense of well-being.

Copyright © Heinle

Chapter 30   Exercise B
Using Semicolons

Combine each of the following sentence groups into one sentence that contains only two independent clauses. Use a semicolon to separate the two clauses. You may need to add, delete, relocate, or change some words; keep experimenting until you find the arrangement that best conveys the meaning of the group of sentences. Your answers may vary from the model answer.

Example: In the springtime, birds nest in the fir tree in my back yard. I see fluttering chickadees. I see bold cardinals.

              In the springtime, birds nest in the fir tree in my backyard; I see fluttering chickadees and bold cardinals.

1. Television soap operas provide a diversion to real life. Soap opera characters are often wealthy. The never seem to work.

_____

_____

2. Ads on afternoon soap operas are directed primarily toward women. The viewer rarely sees ads for men on afternoon soap operas. These ads include soap, toothpaste, skin creams, and nail products.

_____

_____

Chapter 30   Exercise C
Using Semicolons

Combine each of the following sentence groups into one sentence that contains only two independent clauses. Use a semicolon to separate the two clauses. You may need to add, delete, relocate, or change some words; keep experimenting until you find the arrangement that best conveys the meaning of the group of sentences. Your answers may vary from the model answer.

Example: In the springtime, birds nest in the dogwood tree in my back yard. I see fluttering chickadees. I see bold cardinals.

In the springtime, birds nest in the dogwood tree in my backyard; I see fluttering chickadees and bold cardinals.

1. Hale-Bopp was an extraordinary comet. It was seen by millions of ordinary people. It was visible at sunrise and sunset in the spring of 1997 throughout the United States.

_____

_____

2. The United States Capitol is at one end of the Mall. The Washington Monument is at the other end. Both visitors and residents use the space between the two for volleyball, sunbathing, and strolling.

_____

_____

Chapter 30   Exercise D
Using Semicolons

Combine each of the following sentence groups into one sentence that includes a series of items separated by semicolons. You may need to add, delete, relocate, or change words. Try several versions of each sentence until you find the most effective arrangement.

Example: The flag of each Scandinavian country depicts a cross on a solid background. Denmark's flag is red with a white cross. Norway's flag is also red, but its cross is blue, outlined in white. Sweden's flag is blue with a yellow cross.

The flag of each Scandinavian country depicts a cross on a solid background: Denmark's flag is red with a white cross; Norway's flag is also red, but its cross is blue, outlined in white; and Sweden's flag is blue with a yellow cross.

1. A good dictionary offers definitions of words, including some obsolete and nonstandard words. It provides information about synonyms, usage, and word origins. It also offers information on pronunciation and syllabication.

_____

_____

2. Collecting baseball cards is a worthwhile hobby. It helps children learn how to bargain and trade. It also encourages them to assimilate, evaluate, and compare data about major league ball players. Perhaps most importantly, it encourages them to find role models in the athletes whose cards they collect.

_____

_____

Chapter 31   Exercise A
Using Apostrophes

Insert missing apostrophes in the following sentences.

Example: Its a shame that your ring is lost.

It's a shame that your ring is lost.

1. Im not going out in that blizzard.

2. Have you corrected Karens homework yet?

3. Genes store specializes in mens clothing.

4. Allens store carries only boys clothes.

5. My brother-in-laws job is with the county clerks office.

6. Frances and Englands agreement was offset by Japans secret pact
   with Germany.

7. Watch your Ps and Qs at Grandmas house.

8. Johns condition results entirely from neglect.

9. Bev is going on a weeks vacation.

10. Well go if youll stay with the baby.

Chapter 31   Exercise B
Using Apostrophes

Insert missing apostrophes in the following sentences.

Example: Wheres the monkeys toy?

Where's the monkey's toy?

1. Im just a person who cant say no.

2. The childs role is to play the Spirit of 76.

3. His bachelors degree is from his countrys only university.

4. Tally the Ys here and the Ns there.

5. Oohs and ahs rose from the astonished audience.

6. For an hours labor, Lochlin earned a days pay.

7. I wanted to hear yess, but all I heard were maybes.

8. Does Sarah know her ABCs already?

9. The Cowarts home is just around the corner.

10. Amys apartment is upstairs; Jessicas is downstairs.

11. What will the class of 73 plan for the reunion?

12. The five partners signatures were necessary.

13. Shes home, but hes working at a childrens camp.

14. "Well, well have to honor his last will if were to divide the estate
now," said the attorney.

Chapter 32   Exercise A
Using Quotation Marks

Insert missing quotation marks or other related punctuation in the sentences that follow.

1. Where do you think you're going she demanded.

2. Yogi Berra said It ain't over till its over.

3. "A Philmont Experience" is the cover story in the June edition of *Scouter Magazine.*

4. Can you Yanks tell me said the British officer where to find your commanding officer

5. Hemingways *Men without Women* included the story In Another Country.

6. Dover Beach is one of Matthew Arnold's best-known poems.

7. Who said Yes

8. Open your blue books said the professor and begin your exam.

9. The rain has ruined our ski trip complained Megan.

10. We will meet again in two weeks said the professor as the class began to leave.

Chapter 32   Exercise B
Using Quotation Marks

Add single and double quotation marks to these sentences where necessary to set off direct quotations from identifying tags.

Example: Gertrude Stein said, You are all the lost generation.

             Gertrude Stein said, "You are all the lost generation."

1. Freedom of speech does not guarantee anyone the right to yell Fire! in a crowded theater, she explained.

2. To many freshmen, social security means a date for Saturday night.

3. Wordsworth's phrase splendour in the grass was used as the title of a movie about young lovers.

4. *Beside* means next to, but *besides* means except.

5. If everyone will sit down, the teacher announced, the exam will begin.

Chapter 33   Exercise A
Using Other Punctuation Marks

Circle the correct punctuation mark given in the parentheses.

1. I have never been to England (; / :) it is supposed to be lovely.

2. It is lovely in three seasons (; / :) spring, summer, and fall.

3. Winter is not so lovely (; / :) it is cold and windy then.

4. It may be cold, and it may snow (; / :) nevertheless, I can have fun in the winter.

5. In winter I enjoy the following (; / :) skiing, skating, and tobogganing.

6. I also like summer sports (; / :) swimming, riding, hiking.

7. Winter in England is the time for sleigh rides (; / :) summer is the time for hayrides.

8. I used to enjoy staying home (; / :) now I would like to travel.

9. I would enjoy visiting many lands (; / :) France, England, Italy, Norway, Switzerland.

10. There are two pleasures to traveling (; / :) seeing new faces, and visiting new places.

Chapter 33   Exercise B
Using Other Punctuation Marks

Correct any errors in the use of semicolons or colons. Insert your corrections within the paragraph.

The team was in trouble, it had dropped from first place to last in three weeks. The manager called a meeting of the players at which the following issues were discussed; the importance of developing a winning attitude, whereby the players would place the goals of the team over their individual achievements, the imposition of a strict curfew so that the players would be well rested for the games, the problem of teammates competing among themselves for higher salaries and greater coverage in the newspapers, and last but not least, the general lack of hustle and determination on the part of the team's stars.

Chapter 33   Exercise C
Using Other Punctuation Marks

Add dashes where needed in the following sentences.

Example: World War I called "the war to end all wars" was, unfortunately, no such thing.

World War I—called "the war to end all wars"—was, unfortunately, no such thing.

1. Tulips, daffodils, hyacinths, lilies all of these beautiful flowers

grow from bulbs.

2. St. Kitts and Nevis two tiny island nations are now independent

after 360 years of British rule.

3. "But it's not" She paused abruptly and reconsidered her words.

4. He considered several different majors history, English, political

science, and business before deciding on journalism.

5. The two words added to the Pledge of Allegiance in the 1950s

"under God" remain part of the Pledge today.

Chapter 33   Exercise D
Using Other Punctuation Marks

Add parentheses where needed in the following sentences.

Example: The greatest battle of the War of 1812 the Battle of New
            Orleans was fought after the war was declared over.

            The greatest battle of the War of 1812 (the Battle of New
            Orleans) was fought after the war was declared over.

1. George Orwell's *1984* 1949 focuses on the dangers of a totalitarian

   society.

2. The final score 56-0 was a devastating blow for the Wildcats.

3. Hoyt told us that Belize formerly British Honduras offers

   spectacular off-shore diving opportunities.

4. The first phonics book *Phonics Is Fun* has a bright blue cover.

5. Some high school students participate in so many extracurricular

   activities band, sports, drama club, and school newspaper, for

   instance that they have little time to study.

163

Chapter 33   Exercise E
Using Other Punctuation Marks

Add appropriate punctuation—colons, dashes, parentheses, brackets, or slashes—to the following sentences. Be prepared to explain why you chose the punctuation marks. Write your changes in or between the lines.

Example: There was one thing she was sure of if she did well at the interview, the job would be hers.

There was one thing she was sure of: If she did well at the interview, the job would be hers.

1. Mark Twain Samuel L. Clemens made the following statement "I can live for two months on a good compliment."

2. Saudi Arabia, Oman, Yemen, Qatar, and the United Arab Emirates all these are located on the Arabian Peninsula.

3. John Adams 1735-1826 was the second president of the United States; John Quincy Adams 1767-1848 was the sixth.

4. The sign said "No tresspassing *sic*."

Chapter 33   Exercise F
Using Other Punctuation Marks

Add appropriate punctuation—colons, dashed, parentheses, brackets, or slashes—to the following sentences. Be prepared to explain why you chose the punctuation marks. Write your changes in or between the lines.

Example: There was one thing she was sure of if she did well at the interview, the job would be hers.

There was one thing she was sure of: If she did well at the interview, the job would be hers.

1. *Checkmate* a term derived from the Persian phrase meaning "the king" is dead announces victory in chess.

2. The following people were present at the meeting the president of the board of trustees, three trustees, and twenty reporters.

3. Before the introduction of the potato in Europe, the parsnip was a major source of carbohydrates in fact, it was a dietary staple.

4. Liza Minnelli, the actress singer who starred in several films, is the daughter of Judy Garland.

Review Exercise A for Chapters 28–33
Understanding Punctuation

On your own paper, rewrite the following passage, inserting or revising periods, commas, exclamation points, question marks, and quotation marks.

Three men were stationed in the farthest reaches of Alaska, and their supply of orange juice was running low. Two of the men felt that they could take advantage of the third, so they told him to go out into the blizzard and buy some more orange juice in the nearest town. The third man said I will go only if you promise to save the last drop of this remaining orange juice for me. Don't worry the others said we promise. I will definitely not go if you drink that last drop the third man said. We promise, we promise, the others assured him. With that, the third man left. A day went by Two days went by A week and then two weeks went by. The two men figured that the third must have died in the blizzard so they decided "to drink the last bit of orange juice." They took the bottle from the refrigerator, said Cheers, and were about to indulge when the third man flung the door open. I told you he announced I wasn't going to go if you drank that last drop!

Review Exercise B for Chapters 28–33

Understanding Punctuation

On your own paper, rewrite the following paragraphs so that they are properly punctuated.

Small towns and cities especially older ones face difficult financial problems Their revenues are limited but they're expected to maintain service levels despite added costs Sometimes the size of a towns annual budget is restricted by the state in other cases the local officials determine its size Ultimately such budgets are limited by the ability and willingness of citizens to pay the property taxes that generally fund such municipalities.

When a municipal budget is strained officials have two choices increase revenues or cut expenditures In the past extra funds came from the state and federal governments but now many towns must do without such aid Instead increased revenues can come only from new homes whose owners pay property taxes new or revitalized businesses whose tax bills rise with their revenues or new industry whose taxes are a function of space occupied and revenues.

In an older town however with little vacant land not much new growth can be encouraged In addition revitalizing an old run down business district requires time capital and community support Thus if revenues cant or dont grow towns have no choice but to cut their expenses.

How can a town or small city spend less One city manager summed up the problem when he said Were like a business during tough times We have to be more efficient more careful with our pennies and more concerned about our customers the demanding overburdened taxpayers who depend on our services And how does a town accomplish this Few communities have long-term answers for many fixed costs pensions utilities insurance and the like are beyond their control.

Chapter 34   Exercise A
Spelling

Write "C" if the word is correctly spelled. If it is misspelled, write it correctly in the space provided.

1. Wendsday   _____

2. arrangment   _____

3. couragously   _____

4. simular   _____

5. applyed   _____

6. potatos   _____

7. admitance   _____

8. hinderence   _____

9. athelete   _____

10. kindergarden   _____

11. exaduration   _____

12. suprize   _____

13. enterance   _____

14. eventhough   _____

Copyright © Heinle

Chapter 34   Exercise B
Spelling

Underline the correctly spelled word in the parentheses.

1. Jonna will not (except/accept) his present.

2. Vince's hard work (affected/effected) his grades.

3. Raleigh is the (capital/capitol) city of North Carolina.

4. Don't just (lay/lie) there; hop up and answer the phone.

5. To Jim's surprise, no one was (their/there).

6. We allow no (acception/exception) to this rule.

7. Did you (lose/loose) your wallet?

8. Don't forget to renew your driver's (license/lisense).

9. (Driveing/Driving) without one is a crime.

10. If you have renewed it (already/allready), don't worry.

11. Don't drive without it in your (posession/possession).

12. Some (friendly/freindly) officer might ask to see it.

Chapter 35   Exercise A
Capitalization

Correct any capitalization errors—lower-case letters that should be capitals or capitals that should be lower case.

                    aunt   February
Example: My Aunt always gets depressed in february.

1. The Professor who taught english 202 changed my attitude about

   reading the Poetry of alexander pope and robert frost.

2. Swedish tennis pro Bjorn Borg, who won the wimbledon title that

   year, lost the U.S. Open Championship at flushing meadow

   stadium.

3. When Whitney was at harvard, I used to take the amtrak train to

   Boston every friday to visit her.

4. The statue of liberty was closed when i was in new york, but i still

   took the Ferry boat to ellis island.

5. The Articles of Confederation preceded the constitution of the

   United States and the bill of rights.

Chapter 35   Exercise B
Capitalization

Correct any capitalization errors—lower-case letters that should be capitals or capitals that should be lower case.

Lucky Chance Grill

Example: Working at the lucky chance grill has educated me

human nature
about Human Nature.

1. When Fall arrives, the children—angela, erica, beth, and brian—begin to plan for halloween.

2. We drove up maple street until we came to the Highway and turned North toward cumberland state park.

3. Professor andrew luke thomas explained that Siddhartha, called the buddha, founded buddhism in india.

4. Many americans faced hard times when the roaring twenties gave way to the great depression.

5. Our assignment is to read george eliot's *middlemarch*.

6. The mayflower compact established a government for plymouth colony.

7. On a clear Summer evening, we can see the big dipper in the sky.

Chapter 36   Exercise A
Italics

Underline any words that should be italicized.

Example: Year after year, new parents turn to Dr. Spock's <u>Baby and Child Care</u>.

1. Because it is extremely challenging, William Faulkner's The Sound and the Fury is one of those novels that I have enjoyed reading multiple times.

2. Lincoln first gave his Gettysburg Address at the dedication of a cemetery.

3. For many people, the word cavalry is a tongue twister.

4. When the Supreme Court decided Marbury v. Madison, it established the right of judicial review.

5. The hero of Beowulf, a long epic poem in Old English, dies fighting a dragon.

6. The Thinker is Rodan's best-known sculpture.

7. When Sesame Street was first broadcast, it challenged conventional ideas about children's television.

8. The drama group presented Shakespeare's Romeo and Juliet in modern dress.

9. She can call him or vice versa.

10. Cyperus papyrus was used in ancient Egypt for fuel, food, fabric, and paper.

Copyright © Heinle

Name _____ Date _____ Score_____

Chapter 36   Exercise B
Italics

Underline any words that should be italicized.

Example: Year after year, new parents turn to Dr. Spock's <u>Baby and</u>
            <u>Child Care</u>.

1. I always have trouble pronouncing the word schism.
2. He wrote there, but he meant their.
3. She call is strombis pugilis; I call it a pretty shell.
4. I read the Los Angeles Times every day, but I also like the weekly coverage in Newsweek.
5. Stadman's article on Dutch Protestantism appeared in the Sixteenth Century Journal.
6. A similar argument, "Patterns of Worship in Flanders," appeared in Renaissance Studies.
7. An Atlantic crossing on a Concorde is nothing like one was on the Mayflower.
8. The word canteen, derived from the Italian cantina, has been used in English since the eighteenth century.
9. The giant panda, Ailuropoda melanoleuca, is related not to the bear but to the raccoon.
10. The choir presents Handel's Messiah each year.

Chapter 37   Exercise A
Hyphens

Form compound adjectives from the following word groups, inserting hyphens where necessary.

Example: a contract for three years

a three-year contract

1. a relative who has long been lost

2. someone who is addicted to video games

3. a salesperson who goes from door to door

4. a display calculated to catch the eye

5. friends who are dearly beloved

6. a household that is centered on the child

7. a line of reasoning that is hard to follow

8. the border between Tennessee and Kentucky

9. a candidate who is forty-four years old

10. a computer that is friendly to its users

Chapter 37   Exercise B
Hyphens

Add hyphens to the compounds in these sentences wherever they are necessary. Consult a dictionary if necessary.

Example: Alaska was the forty ninth state to join the United States.

            Alaska was the forty-ninth state to join the United States.

1. My pre certification class has fifty three students on the roster, but only thirty seven have shown up.

2. By emphasizing her position as a middle of the road independent, the little known candidate hopes to win the runoff.

3. One of the restaurant's blue plate specials is chicken fried steak.

4. Both Texas and Virginia are right to work states.

5. Don stood on tiptoe to see the near perfect statue, which was well hidden by the security fence.

6. The new store in the mall has a self service makeup counter and stocks many up to the minute gadgets.

7. The so called Saturday night special is opposed by pro gun control groups.

8. For his pre-game meal, he ordered two all beef patties with special sauce, lettuce, cheese, pickles, and onions on a sesame seed bun for his pre game meal.

9. Although last night's speaker presented some thought provoking insights, he hardly presented any earth shattering conclusions.

10. The Braves Mets game was rained out, so the long suffering fans left for home.

Chapter 38   Exercise A
Abbreviations

In the space provided below each sentence, correct any abbreviations that should be spelled out or any words that would be abbreviated in an essay.

1. Of the three bros., Wm. Collins, Junior, is obviously tallest, standing 6 ft. 11 ins. in his stocking feet.

   _____

2. In his address to the Corps of Cadets last Thurs., Gen. Ross announced a 12% increase in dessert expenditures.

   _____

3. Although Meg mailed the two letters on the same day at an Atlanta post office, she was surprised that one letter arrived in CA two days before the other arrived in FL.

   _____

4. The phone calls for Ms. Davis came from Prof. Bollman in NY, from Sen. Nelson in Washington, District of Columbia, and from Gov. Andrews in AZ.

   _____

   _____

5. After taking my bus. admin. final exam, I returned to my dorm room & found a note that read, "See you this aft. when yr. tests are thru."

   _____

   _____

Copyright © Heinle

Chapter 38   Exercise B
Abbreviations

In the space provided below each sentence, correct any abbreviations that should be spelled out or any words that would be abbreviated in an essay.

1. Saint Valentine, martyred c. 270, is remembered thru-out the world each year on Feb. 14.

   _____

2. When it is 1 p.m. EST, it is only 11 a.m. MST.

   _____

3. With her M.A., Beth intends to teach at the local jr. coll. for a few years, but she hopes to earn her doctorate so she can move to a major univ. near her hometown in TN.

   _____

   _____

4. That section of Intro. to Shakespeare meets Mon., Wed., & Fri. at 11 a.m. in the Gabehart Memorial Bldg.

   _____

   _____

5. Today I have anthro. at 8 a.m., but my 10 a.m. lit. course has been canceled, so I hope to get some Xmas shopping done before I work my aft. noon shift.

   _____

   _____

Chapter 39   Exercise A
Numbers

In the space provided below each sentence, correct any numbers that are not treated according to the conventions for nonscientific writing.

1. Including taxes, the price came to nine thousand five hundred twenty dollars and thirty-four cents.

   _____

2. My office number is two thirty-four; I'm usually there and working at the computer by nine a.m.

   _____

3. In eighteen hundred cc of nitrogen, we dissolved three hundred fifty-four point nine gm of liquid sodium.

   _____

4. Physics one twenty-five meets on Thursday mornings.

   _____

5. On page six, the author cites a 12 percent increase in revenues for fiscal year nineteen hundred seventy-one.

   _____

6. The experiment began at six-oh-six; 15 cc were added to the solution every 5 minutes.

   _____

Copyright © Heinle

Chapter 39   Exercise B
Numbers

In the space provided below each sentence, correct any numbers that are not treated according to the conventions for nonscientific writing.

1. Lindsay moved from twelve Sycamore Lane to Sixteen-B Windsor Road, just past Interstate Seventy-Five.

   _____

2. On June eight, nineteen hundred eighty-five, I made my final tuition payment of five hundred forty-seven dollars.

   _____

3. Dinner will be served about 7.

   _____

4. Breakfast ends at exactly nine a.m.

   _____

5. Of the 619 names on the mailing list, 309 submitted the questionnaire by the deadline (which was March nine, 1998), but only twenty-two responded to every question.

   _____

6. The restaurant is at 77 17th Avenue; I'll plan to meet you there no later than 1 o'clock on April sixth, 1990.

   _____

Name _____ Date _____ Score_____

Review Exercise A for Chapters 34–39
Spelling and Mechanics

Read the following sentences, looking for errors in spelling, capitalization, and hyphenation, and for misuse of italics, abbreviations, and numbers. In the space provided, write corrected forms of the following sentences.

1. After Mr Campbell asked for a dozen workers to assist with the Craft Fair at the nursing home, over 30 members of boy scout troop 172 volunteered because they enjoyed working with the residents at last year's event.

_____

_____

_____

_____

2. The scouts also know that mr campbell will reward them by cooking his specialty—Turkey and dressing dinner—on the next camping trip.

_____

_____

_____

Copyright © Heinle

3. The 3 wk unit of study culminated with Mr Hansard's dramatic reading of tennyson's famous poem, *The Charge of the Light Brigade*, accompanied by the overture from the Rossini's opera, William Tell.

_____

_____

_____

_____

4. When Mr Estabrook announced the expenses for last month's camporee (sixty five thousand eight hundred and fifty dollars), Mr Flerchinger was so startled that he almost fell out of his chair.

_____

_____

_____

_____

Name _____ Date _____ Score_____

Review Exercise B for Chapters 34–39
Spelling and Mechanics

Read the following sentences, looking for errors in spelling, capitalization, and hyphenation, and for misuse of italics, abbreviations, and numbers. In the space provided, write corrected forms of the following sentences.

1. Although the calendar said January, it was a surprisingly warm, spring like thurs. morning—January 28th, to be exact—and all andrew could think about was how he would celebrate his birthday with his brothers.

_____

_____

_____

_____

2. Luke earned a four year scholarship to the Fla. public college of his choice; his goal is to earn an m.a. & then choose a grad. school where he can earn a Doctorate.

_____

_____

_____

Copyright © Heinle

3. One of the most famous of eighteenth century literary pieces is Jonathan swift's gulliver's travels, which we read in our English Two-Eighteen class last semester.

_____

_____

_____

_____

4. The local teachers' union negotiated an excellent contract; each teacher will have twenty seven paid holidays—including two weeks during the christmas break; one week for the easter break; and her birthday, plus the day before and the day after.

_____

_____

_____

_____

Chapter 40   Exercise A
Ten Habits of Successful Students

Use the chart below to create a weekly schedule. Make sure to include all of your scheduled hours and time for studying.

	Monday	Tuesday	Wednesday	Thursday	Friday	Saturday	Sunday
5:00 AM							
6:00 AM							
7:00 AM							
8:00 AM							
9:00 AM							
10:00 AM							
11:00 AM							
12:00 PM							
1:00 PM							
2:00 PM							
3:00 PM							
4:00 PM							
5:00 PM							
6:00 PM							
7:00 PM							
8:00 PM							
9:00 PM							
10:00 PM							
11:00 PM							
12:00 PM							

Chapter 40   Exercise B
Ten Habits of Successful Students

Consider the ten questions summarized on pages 447-448 of *The* Brief *Handbook*. List and explain at least five ways you can improve your skills as a student.

1. _____

_____

2. _____

_____

3. _____

_____

4. _____

_____

5. _____

_____

Chapter 41   Exercise A
Developing Active Reading Skills

Consult the Highlighting Symbols Checklist found in Chapter 41 of
The Brief *Holt Handbook*, Select the highlighting methods that you
consider most appropriate. Then highlight the following passage in a
manner that would help you review it, if the need should arise.

One of the more intriguing literary legends surrounding the King
James Version of the Bible alleges that Shakespeare's hand is present
in the 46th Psalm. Turn to the psalm to see for yourself. Count to the
forty-sixth word from the beginning of the psalm (*shake*) and then
identify the forty-sixth word from the end of the psalm (*spear*). These
findings might be dismissed as merely interesting coincidence. The
situation becomes even more intriguing, however, when we realize that
Shakespeare was forty-six years old when the revision was underway in
1610. We shouldn't be surprised to find that Shakespeare played a role
in translating this magnificently poetic portion of the King James
Version.

Chapter 41   Exercise B
Developing Active Reading Skills

Consult the Using Highlighting Symbols Checklist found in Chapter 41 of *The* Brief *Holt Handbook*. Select the highlighting methods that you consider most appropriate. Then highlight the following passage in a manner that would help you review it, if the need should arise.

Giorgio Vasari, the Italian art historian who lived during the sixteenth century, records an interesting anecdote concerning Leonardo's *The Last Supper*. For his models of the disciples, Leonardo drew from life, encountering difficulty only in locating a suitable Judas Iscariot. Throughout much of his work on the painting, Leonardo was troubled by the prior of Santa Maria, who monitored the work's progress from a vantage uncomfortably close for the artist. Upon hearing that the prior had expressed his concerns to Duke Sforza, Leonardo mentioned that any delay he had experienced was merely the result of his having encountered difficulty in identifying a model for the betrayer. But, Leonardo pointed out, he would be delayed no longer, for he had located his model: the prior would serve nicely.

Chapter 42   Exercise A
Writing Essay Examinations

Read each of the following essay examination questions and determine what the key words and important terms in each question are. Write the words in the lines below the question.

1. Define second-wave feminism, trace its history, and explain why it was so popular among middle-class white women. Use specific examples to support your argument.

   _____

   _____

2. Compare and contrast modern and post-modern literature. Identify at least three influential literary works in each movement.

   _____

   _____

3. Briefly summarize human-cloning. Do you support or oppose human-cloning? Justify your answer.

   _____

   _____

4. Summarize the Second Amendment to the United States Constitution. Is this amendment still relevant considering the changes that have taken place since the eighteenth century? Defend your answer.

   _____

   _____

Chapter 42   Exercise B
Writing Essay Examinations

Select one of the essay examination topics found in Exercise A. Compose the topic sentence that you might use to begin your essay response. Then, develop a quick list of the major points you plan to make.

_____

_____

_____

_____

_____

_____

_____

_____

_____

_____

Chapter 43   Exercise A
Writing about Literature

Assume that your instructor has assigned an essay in which you are to provide a summary of the scholarly comments that have been written about *Hamlet* during the past ten years. Identify five credible sources that you would consider appropriate for your purposes.

1. _____

2. _____

3. _____

4. _____

5. _____

Chapter 43   Exercise B
Writing about Literature

Assume that your instructor has assigned an essay in which you are to provide a summary of the scholarly comments that have been written about *Hamlet* during the past ten years. Identify five unworthy sources that you would consider inappropriate for your purposes.

1. _____

2. _____

3. _____

4. _____

5. _____

Chapter 44   Exercise A
Document Design and Manuscript Format

Assume that you are beginning the final version of your essay for submission. The area below is intended to represent the initial page of your essay. Based on the MLA Manuscript Guidelines, provide the appropriate information that would appear atop the first page, plus the title and the essay's first sentence. For your convenience, lines have been provided.

Chapter 44   Exercise B
Document Design and Manuscript Format

Assume that you are preparing for submission the Works Consulted page that will serve as page 6 when it accompanies your essay. The area below is intended to represent the Works Consulted page for your essay. Based on the MLA Manuscript Guidelines, provide the appropriate information that would appear atop the Works Consulted page, plus the first three entries. For your convenience, lines have been provided.

Chapter 45   Exercise A
Writing for the Workplace

Think of a job that you would like to have ten years after you complete your college education. In the space below, provide a letter of application in the semiblock format. Continue the letter on the back of this page.

_____

_____

_____

_____

_____

_____

_____

_____

_____

Chapter 45   Exercise A (continued)
Writing for the Workplace

Continue the letter of application in the space below.

_____

_____

_____

_____

_____

_____

_____

_____

_____

_____

_____

Name _____ Date _____ Score_____

Chapter 45   Exercise B
Writing for the Workplace

In the space below, provide a sample résumé in chronological order to accompany the letter of application you created in Exercise A. Continue the résumé on the back of this page.

_____

_____

_____

_____

_____

_____

_____

_____

_____

_____

Copyright © Heinle

Chapter 45   Exercise B (continued)
Writing for the Workplace

Continue the résumé in the space below.

_____

_____

_____

_____

_____

_____

_____

_____

_____

_____

_____

Review Exercise A for Chapters 40–45
College Survival Skills

Prepare a personalized list of the most important considerations as you prepare for an essay examination.

1. _____

2. _____

3. _____

4. _____

5. _____

Copyright © Heinle

Review Exercise B for Chapters 44–45
College Survival Skills

Prepare a personalized list of the most important considerations as you prepare to submit an essay.

1. _____

2. _____

3. _____

4. _____

5. _____

Chapter 46   Exercise A
Making Oral Presentations

Use the questions below to help you create your oral presentation.

Briefly describe your topic.

_____

_____

_____

_____

How well does your audience know the field or subject you are discussing?

_____

_____

_____

_____

What is the purpose of your presentation?

_____

_____

_____

_____

How much time do you have to deliver your presentation?

_____

_____

_____

Chapter 46   Exercise A (continued)
Making Oral Presentations

How much research do you need to conduct and how long will it take you?

_____

_____

_____

_____

What research resources will you use?

_____

_____

_____

_____

Develop a clear and specific thesis statement that will guide you through the planning stage.

_____

_____

_____

_____

Chapter 46   Exercise B
Making Oral Presentations

When giving an oral presentation it is very important to have developed clear points that you would like to discuss. Use the space below to develop three main points for your presentation. Then, list potential research sources that will help support each point.

Point One:

_____

_____

Research Sources for Support:

_____

_____

Point Two:

_____

_____

Research Sources for Support:

_____

_____

Point Three:

_____

_____

Research Sources for Support:

_____

_____

Copyright © Heinle

Chapter 47   Exercise A
English for Speakers of Other Languages
Using Articles with Nouns

Determine if an article is needed to make the sentences below grammatically correct (a, an, the). If an article is needed, rewrite the sentence
in its correct form. If not, write the letter "C" in the space provided.

When you come over, please bring me book.

_____

_____

Study abroad office will help you complete the proper paperwork for
your trip.

_____

_____

Successful students always set clear, tangible goals.

_____

_____

Students are often required to purchase computer when they enroll in
college.

_____

_____

Melinda told Elena that receiving the award was clearly honor.

_____

_____

Chapter 47   Exercise B
English for Speakers of Other Languages
Using Other Determiners with Nouns

Each sentence below requires the addition of a determiner (this, that, these, those) to make it grammatically correct. Rewrite each sentence using the right determiner.

I wish you would put _____ plate back in the cupboard.

_____

_____

Please put _____ flowers in a nice vase.

_____

_____

Are _____ earrings yours or are they Marcie's?

_____

_____

Generally, Alan keeps _____ books on his desk.

_____

_____

_____ movie is one of my favorites.

_____

_____

Copyright © Heinle

Chapter 47   Exercise C
English for Speakers of Other Languages

No pronouns are present in the following passage. The repetition of the nouns would seem strange to a native speaker of English. On your own paper, rewrite the passage, replacing as many of the nouns as possible with appropriate pronouns. Be sure that the connection between the pronoun and the noun it replaces is clear.

The young couple seated across from Daniel at the dinner the night before were newlyweds from Tokyo. The young couple and Daniel ate together with other guests of the inn at long, low tables in a large dining room. The man introduced himself immediately in English, shook Daniel's hand firmly, and, after learning that Daniel was not a tourist but a resident working in Osaka, gave Daniel a business card. The man had just finished college and was working at the man's first real job, clerking in a bank. Even in a sweatsuit, the man looked ready for the office: chin closely shaven, bristly hair neatly clipped, nails clean and buffed. After a while, the man and Daniel exhausted the man's store of English and drifted into Japanese.

The man's wife, shy up until then, took over as the man fell silent. The woman and Daniel talked about the new popularity of hot springs spas in the countryside around the inn, the difficulty of finding good schools for the children the woman hoped to have soon, and the differences between food in Tokyo and Osaka. The woman's husband ate busily with an air of tolerating the woman's prattling. From time to time, the woman refilled the man's beer glass to served the man radish pickles from a china bowl in the middle of the table, and then returned to the conversation.

Name _____ Date _____Score_____

Chapter 47   Exercise D
English for Speakers of Other Languages

In the following passage, identify all the infinitives (*to* _____),
gerunds (_____*ing*), present participles (_____*ing*), and
past participles (___*ed*, _____*t*, or _____*en*).
Define the function of each as either noun or adjective.

The car is the quintessential American possession. The car, not the

home, is the center of American life. Despite its central place in the

mystique of the American Dream, the individually owned home is

actually anti-American in many ways. Owning a car means freedom,

progress, and individual initiative, the most basic American values. To

own a house means rusting pipes and rotting roof beams. Staying in

one place implies stagnation and decay, whereas moving (always "for-

ward") connotes energy, creativity, never-ending youth: "Moss doesn't

grow on a rolling stone." And the way Americans move is in their cars,

their personalized, self-contained, mobile units.

206   Copyright © Heinle

Chapter 47   Exercise E
English for Speakers of Other Languages

Each sentence below is followed by a list of adjectives and adverbs that can be used in the sentence. Place the adjectives and adverbs where they belong in each sentence. Adjectives and adverbs are listed in the order in which they should appear in the sentences.

1. Researchers believe that tests are not reliable.

   (most, now, IQ, entirely)

   _____

2. Just as culture is derived from Greece, culture is derived from China. (European, ancient, Asian, ancient)

   _____

   _____

3. The people of Louisiana play a music called zydeco.
   (Cajun, southern, lively)

   _____

4. According to the Japanese proverb, for a lid there's a pot.
   (old, cracked, chipped)

   _____

Chapter 47   Exercise F
English for Speakers of Other Languages

Each sentence below is followed by a list of adjectives and adverbs that can be used in the sentence. Place the adjectives and adverbs where they belong in each sentence. Adjectives and adverbs are listed in the order in which they should appear in the sentences.

1. Because I transferred credits from my school, I was able to graduate.

   (many, previous, early)

   _____

   _____

2. Often, feminists feel they are describing the condition of women in the world, when they are describing women in America.

   (too, American, all, actually, only)

   _____

   _____

3. Kenjy works hours on essays, but he remembers to take breaks.

   (usually, many, periodic)

   _____

4. When you begin to exercise, start and build up to levels.

   (slowly, steadily, strenuous)

   _____

Copyright © Heinle

Name_____ Date_____ Score_____

Chapter 47   Exercise G
English for Speakers of Other Languages
Word Order

Create yes/no questions from the statements below using the Word Order section in *The* Brief *Handbook* as a guide.

Joey will study hard for his final exams.

_____

_____

Melanie can use web sites as resources for her paper about Mary McCarthy.

_____

_____

Bob often likes to do his homework alone.

_____

_____

The new policy will assist single mothers in the area.

_____

_____

Using a day planner does help you better manage your time.

_____

_____

Chapter 47   Exercise H
English for Speakers of Other Languages
Commonly Confused Words

A number of word pairs in English have similar meanings. Choose between the word pairs in the sentences below. Write your choice on the line beside each sentence.

_____   Matt has (no, not) interest in going to that party.

_____   I realize that you wanted to go swimming today, but Barton Springs is simply (too, very) far away.

_____   There are (much, many) people who simply do not like fried green tomatoes.

_____   Mona has (no, not) finished her resume.

_____   I always work out, (even if, even though) it means missing my favorite television show.

_____   She is a (too, very) methodical person, which makes her an excellent mathematician.

_____   Sheila has (much, many) experience in the ways of human behavior.

_____   There is only a (little, few) soup left, but I'm saving it for Keith.

_____   Paul and Todd continued to run the race (even if, even though) they both wanted to give up.

_____   Karla has (no, not) desire to finish the problem set.

_____   A (few, little) of us are going to go dancing later tonight.

Copyright © Heinle

Chapter 47   Exercise H (continued)
English for Speakers of Other Languages
Commonly Confused Words

_____   (Some, Any) people like to do their research before
                      they begin writing.

_____   I don't have (any, some) ties, so I'll have to go
                      shopping before the ceremony.

_____   (Even if, Even though) Kathy knew she would probably
                      get a C in the class, she decided to take it.

_____   There are (many, much) things I want to know about
                      farming so I've chosen to major in agriculture.

Appendix A   Exercise A
Parts of Speech

Underline the nouns in the following sentences.

Example: Most <u>students</u> go to the weekly <u>dances</u>.

1. In spite of the terrible downpour, 107,000 fans attended the game and stayed until the final buzzer.

2. At the lake last summer, we fished each morning, swam each afternoon, and hiked each evening.

3. The campus bookstore will be open late on Tuesday night, but it will close early on Friday afternoon.

4. The University of North Carolina, located in the town of Chapel Hill, has buildings that date back to colonial days.

5. The fencing team is a small group of dedicated athletes.

6. The newspaper comes out every week and is noted for its lively articles and controversial columns.

7. The crew of the lunar module performed the scheduled tasks and experiments before returning to base.

8. Math exams can be especially challenging for students whose majors are in the humanities.

9. Neil Armstrong was the first person to walk on the moon.

10. Chicken with mashed potatoes is my favorite meal.

Name _____ Date _____ Score_____

Appendix A   Exercise B
Parts of Speech

Underline the correct pronoun in each sentence.

Example: Amy and (<u>she</u>/her) have excellent study habits.

1. They pushed Adam and (I/me) down the hill.

2. The sisters raced to (her/their) treehouse.

3. The Risers and (we/us) plan to camp this weekend.

4. The team's trophy is for (its/its) outstanding sportsmanship.

5. Wanda and (I/me) will give our reports today.

6. (Who/Whom) was looking for me this morning?

7. (Who/Whom) did you meet at the airport?

8. To (who/whom) did you address the letter?

9. The new employees, Beth and (I/me), began the training program immediately.

10. The company's training program was designed for the new employees, Beth and (I/me).

11. Many of (we/us) students take classes and hold jobs.

12. (Him/He) and Margaret made a detailed map of the area.

13. Between you and (I/me), the new boss is great.

14. Jim knows more about zoology than (she/her).

15. Our supervisor encourages Sarah more than (I/me).

Copyright © Heinle   213

Appendix A   Exercise C
Parts of Speech

Underline the correct pronoun in each sentence.

1. They suspected that the prankster was (he/him).

2. I would not want to be (she/her).

3. Neither the general nor the soldier lost (his/their) life.

4. All of us have to do (her/our) jobs in this organization.

5. I left my coat with Fay and (they/them).

6. (We/Us) athletes all went out for the team.

7. My sister and (they/them) are good friends.

8. Who sent this package to (me/myself)?

9. All that confusion was caused by (him/himself).

10. I wish I were as easygoing as (they/themselves).

11. (He and I/Him and me) prefer to listen to classical music.

12. Neither Trish nor Kathy missed (her/their) class.

13. Eight of the plants produced (its/their) flowers as expected.

14. (Who/Whom) is the candidate of your choice?

15. For (who/whom) will you cast your vote?

Name _____ Date _____ Score_____

Parts of Speech

Underline the nouns and pronouns that are examples of the case specified in parentheses for each sentence.

Example: (nominative or subjective) The <u>cat</u> ate the canary.

1. (nominative or subjective) The doctor is the speaker who will appear first.

2. (possessive) Our cat lay on my mother's bed and licked the boy's chewing gum from its paw.

3. (objective) Whom did you invite to the party?

4. (nominative or subjective) We will go there tomorrow.

5. (possessive) The governor's speech astounded many members of his audience.

6. (objective) Give it to them or they'll complain to me.

7. (nominative or subjective) She is as serious as he.

8. (possessive) The police asked whose purse was missing.

9. (nominative or subjective) The brothers, Allen and Gene, live in different states.

10. (possessive) His swimming at noon is a daily ritual.

11. (objective) I sat behind him and her.

12. (possessive) His coat is in their hall closet.

13. (possessive) Dr. Edmundson's lectures are packed with

14. interesting stories.

15. (nominative or subjective) They can't walk far at this hour and in this weather.

Appendix A   Exercise E
Parts of Speech

In the space provided write "C" if the sentence is correct as it stands or "X" if it contains an error in possessive form. Circle and correct the incorrect form.

1. _____ In this group of students, their the innovators.

2. _____ They're opinion is considered important here.

3. _____ Whose the group that presented the asteroid project that won

first place in the contest?

4. _____ Who's turn is it to feed the piranha?

5. _____ The womens' softball team has been undefeated in the last

four tournaments in which it has competed.

Appendix A   Exercise F
Parts of Speech

In the space provided, write "C" if the example has a complete verb or
"I" if it has an incomplete verb.

1. _____   Brian and Beth visited Yosemite National Park.

2. _____   All members of the Beta Club to attend the baseball game.

3. _____   Scouts with flashlights served as guides along the path.

4. _____   What the surgeon told the class of interns.

5. _____   My computer has crashed only once this week.

6. _____   Crashed or froze ten times last week.

7. _____   Most students prefer to purchase used textbooks.

8. _____   Everybody to hurry for shelter.

9. _____   With friends they enjoying the snow.

10. _____   Mike and Diane making snowballs.

11. _____   The wind blowing and chilling.

12. _____   A blizzard might have been coming.

13. _____   Errands to the bank, the post office, and the bakery.

14. _____   Why are all research papers due just before Thanksgiving?

15. _____   The rain in Spain mainly on the plain.

Appendix A   Exercise G
Parts of Speech

Complete each sentence by underlining the appropriate form of the verb in parentheses.

Example: The fisherman (<u>caught</u>/was caught by) the trout.

1. The attorney (reviewed/was reviewed by) the contracts.

2. The dog (combed/was combed by) its trainer.

3. The professor (graded/was graded by) the essays.

4. The church bell (rang/was rung by) the elderly caretaker.

5. The hungry loggers (ate/were eaten by) the pancakes.

6. The pancakes (ate/were eaten by) the hungry loggers.

7. The prize cucumber (grew/was grown by) Cathy Cowart.

8. Amanda (answered/was answered by) every question in the review section at the end of the chapter.

9. Each e-mail submission to the contest (answers/is answered by) the computer, which sends an acknowledgement by return e-mail.

10. When a caller leaves a message, it (records/is recorded by) the answering machine.

11. Occasionally the tape (skips/is skipped by) a message.

12. The cat (has untangled/has been untangled by) the ball of twine.

Appendix A   Exercise H
Parts of Speech

Underline the correct adjective in each sentence.

1. Sarah's hair is naturally (curled/curly).

2. In two pages, write (a/an) history of American film.

3. Brenda looks (tired/tiredly).

4. Reece wears only (sloppy/sloppily) clothes.

5. What an (unsightly/unsighted) mess!

6. Ronnie waited for this (luckily/lucky) break.

7. Caitlin combed her (gold/golden) hair.

8. The strawberry jam is too (sweet/sweetly).

9. Laura stopped at (their/theirs) apartment yesterday.

10. (Each/Both) sheep are ready for shearing.

11. (Each/Both) sheep has its own pedigree.

12. (This/These) crew will report for duty tomorrow.

13. (This/These) crew members are on vacation.

14. The movie had one (tense/tenser) moment after another.

15. Negotiators avoided (a/an) union strike.

Appendix A   Exercise I
Parts of Speech

Underline the adjectives in the following sentences.

1. The staff worked best with a definite deadline.

2. Jessie grabbed her old boots and ran hurriedly.

3. The six dogs ran ahead, playfully romping in the high grass.

4. The trip is rather long, but we usually arrive in two days.

5. We anxiously awaited Mother's call to eat the delicious meal that she had meticulously placed on a beautifully decorated table.

6. Diane carelessly left her blue backpack in the classroom.

7. Very soon the cold water began dripping loudly on the parquet floor in the vacant room.

8. Joel may be quite tall, but he has never played basketball.

9. From their dazed appearance, we concluded that each exhausted hiker was ready for a warm bath, a bowl of hot soup, and a long rest in a cozy bed.

10. In the final competition, the group of four students worked amazingly well together as they addressed each perplexing task that the committee presented.

Appendix A   Exercise J
Parts of Speech

Underline the correct adverb in each sentence.

1. To close the window, turn the crank (gentle/gently).

2. Raise the garage door as (careful/carefully) as possible.

3. Even in the worst weather, Trish is (seldom/seldomly) late.

4. Weeks of practice paid off when the play was executed (perfect/ perfectly) and Beth's team won the game in the final seconds.

5. Don fought (manly/manfully) for his rights.

6. Fay could (usual/usually) run quickly.

7. Erica (rare/rarely) displays anger on the field.

8. Everyone thought (high/highly) of Coach Cowart.

9. Loose gravel convinced them to ride (slow/slowly) on their bikes.

10. In spite of the muddy track, the horse raced (fast/fastly).

11. I enjoy watching the camels running (graceful/gracefully).

12. The children ran (wild/wildly) across the playground.

13. Cathy visited her mother (often/oftenly).

14. The bell rang (more loudly/most loudly) than ever.

15. The green team finished (last/lastly).

Appendix A   Exercise K
Parts of Speech

Underline the adverbs in the following sentences.

1. The staff worked best with a definite deadline.

2. Jessie grabbed her old boots and ran hurriedly.

3. Julie actually knew she would do well on the exam.

4. The dog's heart beat loudly as he panted rapidly.

5. Camille's extremely regal appearance surprised her friends.

6. We sometimes review customer accounts randomly.

7. The six dogs ran ahead, playfully romping in the high grass.

8. Stomach pains are most often caused by overeating.

9. They danced gracefully despite the band's mistakes.

10. The trip is rather long, but we usually arrive in two days.

11. We anxiously awaited Mother's call to eat the delicious meal that she had meticulously placed on a beautifully decorated table.

12. Diane carelessly left her blue backpack in the classroom.

13. Very soon the cold water began dripping loudly on the parquet floor in the vacant room.

14. Joel may be quite tall, but he has never played basketball.

15. Claire is unlikely to be home now; try again tomorrow.

Appendix A   Exercise L
Parts of Speech

For each sentence, underline the most logical of the prepositions in parentheses.

1. The balloon descended (above/around/to) the ground.

2. The ten children got along well (in spite of/by way of/between) their age differences.

3. As the children watched helplessly, the ball rolled (with/across/on account of) the concrete driveway.

4. To everyone's amazement, the magician waved his wand and then lofted the rabbit (beyond/in back of/above) his head.

5. (After/Before/Between) the storm left the area, the sky darkened, thunder rumbled, and the rain came down in buckets.

6. (Among/Between/In spite of) you and me, I think this will be an action-packed spring break.

7. At night during the summer months, the city lights cast a spooky glow (within/up to/behind) the dark hill.

8. To the dismay of the judge, the news spread rapidly (between/among/through) the jury members.

9. The monster growled and crept slowly (to/toward/regarding) the cowering heroine.

10. In our neighborhood, the Sunday newspaper always arrives (until/during/before) 8:15 A.M.

Appendix A   Exercise M
Parts of Speech

Underline the prepositions in the following sentences.

1. At the beginning of the term, the bookstore is not an enjoyable place to visit because it is too crowded.

2. Despite being excited about new courses, students are needlessly exhausted by the lines at the bookstore.

3. All the books are arranged under the names of the departments, so I had to make several stops to find mine.

4. When other students blocked the aisles, I had to push by to get to the right place to find my books.

5. The books for my English course were on the top shelf.

6. To get them, I had to climb up on a ladder that was shaking because of the jostling crowd.

7. My fear of heights, however, was less than my fear of being trampled when I found my math books on the bottom shelf, behind those for calculus.

8. After my books were gathered up, I saw that the lines for the cashiers wound behind the sweatshirts and in front of the dictionaries.

9. I stood in line for an hour, thumbing through my books and talking with other students during the wait.

10. At last I had my books and was ready to practice my weight lifting on the long walk back to my room.

11. My mom thinks I'm too much of a complainer, but what does she know about life at college?

Appendix A   Exercise N
Parts of Speech

Complete the sentences below by filling in the most logical prepositions from the following list.

against	at	during	in	into
of	on	under	with	

Example: The Gunpowder Plot occurred <u>on</u>
            November 5, 1605.

1. _____ that time of religious strife, King James I
   ruled England, a Protestant country.

2. _____ November 5, he was to open Parliament
   with a formal ceremony.

3. The plan of the Catholic conspirators was to blow up Parliament
   _____that time.

4. Then they expected their fellow English Catholics to rise up
   _____ the Protestant government that suppressed
   their religion.

5. To carry out their plot, the conspirators had rented a cellar
   _____ Westminster, where the House of Lords
   met.

6. There they had stored thirty-six kegs of gunpowder, covered
   _____ firewood and coal.

7. Some members _____ the House of Lords
   received warning letters, urging them not to attend.

8. The secret cellar was discovered, and one conspirator, Guy Fawkes,
   was arrested when he came _____ the cellar.

9. _____ England, November 5 is still called Guy
   Fawkes Day.

10. _____ that day, fireworks and bonfires
    commemorate the discovery of the plot.

Appendix A   Exercise O
Parts of Speech

Underline the conjunctions in the following sentences.

Example: They were so hungry that they ate <u>not</u> <u>only</u>
the eggs <u>and</u> sausage <u>but</u> <u>also</u> the doughnuts
<u>and</u> coffeecake.

1. Both Carol and Doug enjoy the circus clowns.

2. Either Don will buy the clock, or he will pass up a great offer.

3. Staci and Linda had to wait in the hall until the doors opened.

4. We did our best, whatever happens next.

5. Normally the course has a prerequisite; nevertheless, the professor
may admit a student without it.

6. Unless Beth leaves now, she will miss the return flight.

7. The lectures are twice a week; in addition, students must attend
weekly labs and discussion groups.

8. Erica selected the college because it has a fine reputation.

9. Neither her mother nor her father expected her to call.

10. Morning came, yet the sky remained gray.

11. Call the fire department or the ambulance squad.

12. The police officer assured me that the burglar alarm would
continue to ring unless someone turns it off.

Appendix A   Exercise P
Parts of Speech

Underline the correct conjunction in each sentence.

Example: She eats constantly (and/<u>but</u>) remains thin.

1. (Since/Because) the school was founded, it has offered courses in theology and ethics.

2. The department of religion (and/but) philosophy offers both courses each semester.

3. (While/Once) you wait for your interview, you might want to review the job requirements.

4. I had to take the 8 a.m. section (because/although) that was the only vacant slot in my schedule.

5. She knew when the paper was due; (consequently/nevertheless), she handed it in a week late.

6. He wanted to take a course in nearly every department; (moreover/for example), he thought everyone should read Shakespeare, study philosophy, and review American history.

7. Look in the dining hall (or/but) in the lounge.

8. Neither the regular fire drills (nor/but also) the occasional false alarms had prepared the students for the trauma of the real fire that struck their dorm that stormy winter night.

9. The crocuses were blooming (although/before) snow still covered the ground.

10. The baby refuses to eat (lest/unless) her grandmother feeds her.

Appendix A   Exercise Q
Parts of Speech

Use the conjunctions in parentheses to link the following short sentences or fragments. Rewrite and punctuate as necessary to generate a sentence that is smooth and correct.

Example: You should hurry. We are going to be late. (unless)
            Unless you hurry, we are going to be late.

1. The program aired. The executives had debated whether to release it. (before)

   _____

2. The dining hall serves three meals a day. Students must eat during the serving hours. (however)

   _____

   _____

3. The western cowboy. The frontiersman. Blend truth with American mythology. (both, and)

   _____

4. The administrators. The faculty. Correctly projected enrollment trends. (neither, nor)

   _____

Appendix A   Exercise R
Parts of Speech

Underline the interjections in the following sentences.

1. Wow! Can you imagine how excited Beth was?

2. From the examination room, I heard someone yell, "Ouch!" There's

   no way I'm staying here. I'll see you at home.

3. When I ask Grandma, she always says, "Oh, you're just like your

   father when he was your age."

4. When the mouse ran through the garage, Aunt Alice shouted,

   "Heavens!" and then grabbed the broom.

Appendix B   Exercise A
Sentence Review

In the space provided, write "S" if the example has a subject or "X" if it does not. Underline the simple subjects that you find.

Example: __S__ <u>Everyone</u> liked my new car.

1. _____ More than you will ever know.

2. _____ Forty chairs per classroom.

3. _____ Need several pounds of shrimp.

4. _____ We played cards until after midnight

5. _____ Meg cares about her patients

6. _____ Comprehension and vocabulary.

7. _____ Beyond his limit, Brian took a break.

8. _____ Is running several miles each morning.

9. _____ Love going to the mall.

10. _____ Our vacation was refreshing.

Appendix B   Exercise B
Sentence Review

On your own paper, expand each basic sentence by adding at least a phrase or a clause.

Example: George bought a car.
            George bought a car that he will pick up Monday.

1. The dog barked.

2. Sarah bought a house.

3. I will finish my homework.

4. The food is cooked.

5. The doctor will be back Tuesday.

6. Stop the red car.

7. My brother called.

8. The dean spoke.

9. We began our vacation.

10. My cousin is a lawyer.

11. I rode the trolley.

12. When do you leave?

13. The library is closed.

14. He swam a dozen laps.

15. He played the violin.

Name _____ Date _____ Score_____

Appendix B   Exercise C
Sentence Review

For each of the following sentences, identify the basic sentence pattern. Ignore any added modifiers, phrases, or dependent clauses. Identify the pattern using these abbreviations:

s + v (subject + intransitive verb)

s + v + do (subject + transitive verb + direct object)

s + v + io + do (subject + transitive verb +
                        indirect object + direct object)

s + v + do + oc (subject + transitive verb +
                        direct object + object complement)

s + v + sc (subject + linking verb + subject complement—
                        predicate noun or adjective)
Example:

____S + V + IO + DO____ The mayor pitched Robin the first
                        ball of the season.

1. _____ The cardinals built their nest.

2. _____ The birds fed their babies the worms.

3. _____ The canals on Mars resemble an
                        irrigation system.

4. _____ The class elected Frank.

5. _____ The class elected Frank president.

232   Copyright © Heinle

Appendix B   Exercise D
Sentence Review

For each of the following sentences, identify the basic sentence pattern. Ignore any added modifiers, phrases, or dependent clauses. Identify the pattern using these abbreviations:

s + v (subject + intransitive verb)

s + v + do (subject + transitive verb + direct object)

s + v + io + do (subject + transitive verb +
                 indirect object + direct object)

s + v + do + oc (subject + transitive verb +
                 direct object + object complement)

s + v + sc (subject + linking verb + subject complement—
            predicate noun or adjective)

Example:

   S + V + IO + DO _____ The mayor pitched Robin the first
                                  ball of the season.

1. _____ That solar system disintegrated.

2. _____ The solar system disintegrated years
                         ago.

3. _____ The exam was difficult.

4. _____ The soccer team won.

5. _____ The soccer team won the
                         championship yesterday.

6. _____ The soccer team became the
                         champions.